G STREET CHRONICLES PRESENTS

CITY LIGHTS

GEORGE SHERMAN HUDSON

Cover Design: Oddball Dsgn
             davida@oddballdsgn.com

Typesetting & Ebook Converson:
             G&S Typesetting & Ebook Conversion
             info@gstypesetting.com

LCN: 2011926125
ISBN: 9780983431114

Join us on Facebook G Street Chronicles Fan Page

Acknowledgements

First I would like to thank God for making this possible. I want to acknowledge my loving grandmother, Grandma Walker, for keeping me sane in my trying times.

All the love in the world goes out to my loving parents, Lois and George.

Also much love to my kids who I truly adore; Jazmine, Sherman and Semaj.

Also thanks and much love to the "First Lady of G Street Chronicles" and the best VP in the biz, Shawna A. Grundy…you are one of a kind.

Thanks and much love to Marcel Hill, my little soldier who stood strong. I appreciate you…Tighten up! Also a special thanks to Erica Jones, I appreciate your assistance when I really needed it…you're still my "friend".

Much love to all my family, the Hudson's and the Walkers, it's time for a family reunion! My playa partner and highly anticipated author Khaream Gibson, bro that TWO FACE going to change the game, much love. To all my fam behind the wall: Buckhead, Thad, Mario, Buddy Lee, Money, Cole Heart(Urban Executive Authors), Rick, Champ, Ceelo, Vegas, Tater Head (The Tractor Back Gate King)…too many to name if I forgot you I'll catch you on the next one. To all my G Street Chronicles' family Shawna, Marcel, Mz. Robinson, Khaream, Queen B.G., India, Sa'id, Cole Hart, Ali, Vanessa, Deborah and Charlene…we taking over!!

Dedication

This book is dedicated to all my fam in the struggle.
Sh** get greater later!

THE RISE

The federal agent watched Real get out of his lime green Lamborghini Murcialago LP 460 with his fiancée Constance and head into G-Spot, his high class strip club located on Peachtree Street in downtown Atlanta. Real had been under federal investigation now for six months, ever since a federal informant tipped them off about his illegal activities.

Anyone who came into contact with Real would surely put him well beyond his actual age of only twenty-seven years. He was six feet tall with a medium built muscular frame that the ladies couldn't get enough of. His smooth, charcoal black skin, wavy hair, and light brown eyes gave him an exotic look that would have any woman fawning over him.

Real was a real charmer and a ladies man. He prided himself on his slick tongue and convincing rhetoric. Some people in the past had mistaken his easygoing manner for weakness, but in the end, they found out Real was an extremely dangerous individual.

Constance, Real's baby girl, fiancée, and business partner, was always by his side. Constance was three years older than Real, the spitting image of Lisa Raye with a little more hips and ass. Constance grew up in the College Park projects, where she got down with the grimiest of niggas hustling crack to the project fiends. After a few run-ins with other hustlers, the word spread quickly that lil' fine ass Constance would bust her gun at the drop of a dime.

After graduating from Banneker High, Constance tried her hand at real estate. In no time, she became a highly reputable broker that only dealt in the most high-end homes. Constance became a millionaire virtually overnight.

Constance and Real had met three years earlier at a mutual friend's birthday party. They kept each other company throughout the party. Before leaving the party, they exchanged numbers and promised to stay in contact. A week later, Constance was selling Real a $4.7 million estate in North Atlanta—the one in which they now both reside.

Real was a millionaire in his own right, raking in millions in the drug trade, more than he would ever make going legit. He supplied dealers from every coast. Moving over 100 kilos a week enabled him to live the lifestyle of some of the world's biggest sports figures. After continuous preaching from Constance to put together some kind of legit source of income, he opened up G-Spot, an upscale strip club that catered to the rich and famous.

Real and Constance were on their way to a Tyler Perry play when Real got a call from Max. "Say, cuz," said the manager of G-Spot, "we need your assistance down here. It's very important," Max said firmly.

Max was Real's older cousin. He was discharged from the military right after the Gulf War. As soon as Max heard about his lil' cousin Real starting a strip club, he practically begged him for the managing position. Constance was totally against it, but Real disregarded Constance's wishes and gave his cousin the job anyway. Unfortunately, it took a while for Real to see just how right Constance was.

"I'm on my way," Real said, placing his phone back into the car charger.

"On your way? Where you goin'?" Constance snapped.

"Max needs me down at the club. It's only going to take a

second," Real said, turning the Lambo around and heading back up to the club.

"Man, come on, now! What the hell you hire this nigga for? To watch pussy! Shit, you might as well be managing your own shit! Every night, you get a call to go do his fuckin' job! You need to hire somebody to handle your business so you'll have time to spend with your fuckin' lady!" Constance barked as they pulled up into the club parking lot.

Real knew when it was good to let Constance have her say, especially when she was right, but by the same token, Constance also knew when to hold her tongue.

"Come on," Real told Constance as he opened the door on the Lambo.

Ignoring his command, Constance sat in the car until he walked around, opened up her door, and helped her out of the car. Walking hand in hand, they entered G-Spot.

Chapter 2

" *H*ey, cuz! Two slick-dressed Italian guys demanded to see you. For what, I don't know, but they up in VIP with some of their other friends," Max told Real as he pointed toward the VIP section of the club.

"Italians?" Real repeated, trying to figure out what the men could possibly want. Real didn't know any local Italians.

"Yeah," Max said, looking in their direction.

"What they want?" Constance asked angrily, furious that her night was put on hold by Max—again.

While Constance and Real stood in the middle of the club floor, naked girls spoke to Real and ignored Constance as they walked by. Constance made it known to every girl working that she wouldn't hesitate to fuck them up when it came to Real. Some of the girls respected her situation, but a good majority of them didn't. Every chance one of them got, they would come on to Real in some kind of way. After a while, it was known around the club that Real wasn't going to cheat on Constance, so they stopped trying—all but Cream, the beautiful half-Black, half-White stallion. Cream was determined to break Real down and get him into her bed.

"I told you I don't know what they want," Max snapped looking at Constance with pure hatred.

"So you called us all the way down here, and you don't even know what they want? Did you even ask?" Constance snapped back.

"I called Real down here, not you," Max answered harshly.

"Enough!" Real yelled, leaving Max and Constance standing in the middle of the floor looking at each other as he went to the VIP section to see what the Italians wanted. "Somebody looking for me?" Real asked, looking at the men.

They instantly stopped throwing money at the naked girl and looked up at him. "Who are you?" asked one of the men.

"I'm Real, the owner. Now, who wants to see me?" Real asked again.

"Oh! Real! Come take a seat, my friend," the young, fancy-dressed Italian told Real after making his friend move out of the seat beside him.

"I'm good. What's the problem?" Real asked, still standing staring the man down.

"Oh, there's no problem, my friend. I just came to deliver a very important message from Mr. Rossi," the young Italian said as he stood and walked over to Real.

"Rossi? What's the message?" Real asked, confused. He didn't recognize the name.

The Italian man got up close on Real and whispered, "Mr. Rossi says you work for him or you don't work at all. He knows you are making his competition, the Moretti family, very rich, which is also making Moretti's stronghold on the cartel a lot stronger. Mr. Rossi can't touch Mr. Moretti at this time, but he can touch you. So, what'll it be?" the young Italian asked with a sly smile.

Real placed his arm around the man's shoulder and said firmly, "Tell your boss Mr. Rossi that I said to go fuck himself and that I don't sit well with threats. Now, you and your boys get the fuck up out of my establishment!" Real said, smiling as he exited the VIP section, motioning for Max and Constance to follow.

"What up, cuz?" Max asked as they entered Real's back

office.

"Everything's good. Just some rich, arrogant Italians trying to invest in the club, which is totally out of the question," Real told Max as Constance stood by, picking up on the lie.

"Oh, okay, cuz. I got everything under control. I will call you tomorrow with an update on thangs," Max said, wiping the sweat from his forehead with the back of his hand.

Constance rolled her eyes.

"A'ight, cool," Real said, turning to walk out the office.

"Under control my ass!" Constance uttered as she followed Real out of the back office.

As Real walked across the floor, he noticed the Italians exiting. The tall, lanky one looked in his direction and smiled. Real smiled back.

A few minutes later, Real and Constance were turning out of the G-Spot onto Peachtree Street.

Picking up on Real's different mood, Constance spoke softly. "What's going on, baby?" she asked, sensing his uneasiness.

"Some spic trying to make demands. Had the nerve to send me a message that if I don't work for him, I don't work at all. Can you believe that? Ain't that some shit? He must don't know who the fuck Real is!" Real shouted, getting madder and madder as he thought about the threat from the man in the silky suit.

"Who sent the message?" Constance inquired, trying to see if she recognized the name as one of her wealthy real estate clients. She had sold several high-end homes to Italian drug lords.

"Rossi!" Real spat.

"Hmm. Never heard that name before. So what's next?" Constance asked.

"I'm going to call old man Moretti to see what the deal is. If he don't fix it, I will!" Real snapped.

"He'll straighten it out," Constance said, hoping he would—but even if he didn't, she was going to ride with Real to the very end, no matter what.

"Look, baby, I really ain't in the mood right now for the play. I really need to make some calls," Real said, knowing that she would understand.

"Okay. Me neither," Constance agreed.

Turning around, Real took the Lambo to speeds it had never reached before on the way back home.

Chapter 3

" *B*itch nigga, you better have my eighty grand by the end of the week, or else my people here will be back, and the next time they leave, you won't be fuckin' breathin'!" Cash shouted as his two goons pistol whipped the young dealer.

Cash was Real's good friend and lieutenant. Real had met Cash back in the day on Godby Road. Cash was the true definition of a young hustler. He would stay in the trap all day every day. Seeing the hustle young Cash had and how solid he was made Real take him under his wing. Years later, Cash became very wealthy, all because of Real.

As well as they worked together, Cash was the direct opposite of Real. He was tall, lanky, bald headed, and very unattractive. Known in circles for his pistol play, Cash wouldn't hesitate to unload his clip. At the ripe old age of twenty-four, Cash was considered a legend around town. While Real dealt with the Morettis, Cash and his goons dealt with the streets. Cash knew his position and played it well, with no regrets.

Just as he gave the word for his goons to release the dealer, Cash's cell phone rang. "What up, bro?" he answered when he saw Real's number on the screen.

"I need you to come out to the house ASAP," Real told him firmly.

"Damn, bro, can't it wait until tomorrow? I got Jesse and B-Low riding with me anyway. You know I can't bring them out to your spot," Cash said, watching B-Low and Jesse laughing as the young dealer ran off.

"Look, man, drop them two niggas off and get out here! This is important!" Real snapped and hung up his office phone.

Cash could tell by Real's actions that it was a serious matter, so he hurriedly dropped B-Low and Jesse off and navigated his brand new burgundy 600 SEL Mercedes Benz through the night traffic to Real's house.

A half hour later, Cash was pulling up in front of Real's million-dollar home. Cash was lost for words every time he went out to Real's place. The six-bedroom home sat on ten acres of well-manicured land. Behind the home sat an Olympic-sized swimming pool, full basketball court, tennis court, and guest house. Adjacent to that was a custom-built garage that housed Real's lime green Lamborghini Murcialago LP460, snow white Rolls–Royce drop-head Coupe, and black on black Range Rover Sport. Next to Real's expensive collection were Constance's lavender Bentley GTC, bright cherry red H-2, and midnight blue Ferrari 360 Spider that she barely drove.

Cash stepped out of his Benz into the cold night air.

Ding! Ding!

A few seconds after ringing the bell, Constance appeared at the door. "Hey, Cash," she said. "Come on in. Real's down in his office." She stepped aside, letting Cash in.

"What's up, sis? You good?" Cash asked as he entered.

"Just fine. Just see what's up with Real," she told him as she closed the door behind them.

"All the time," Cash replied as he hurried through the house to Real's home office.

On the way to Real's office, Cash thought back on the times when Real had stayed in a humble two-bedroom condo out in College Park. Now, his crib had marble floors, two full kitchens, an elevator, three fire places, and a bad ass home theatre. *Man, my boy's come a long way,* Cash thought to himself. "What's up, bro?' Cash asked as he entered Real's office.

"A lil' problem from the cartel," Real answered, rearing back into his oversized leather desk chair.

"What kind of problem?" Cash sat down in the oversized office chair positioned in front of the desk.

"A couple Italians came down to the club tonight with a message from a Mr. Rossi. This Rossi says I work for him or don't work at all."

"Work for him or don't work at all!" Cash spat.

"Yeah. He got to be playing!" Real fired back.

"Who the fuck this wetback think he is? He don't run shit!" Cash yelled as he jumped out of the office chair and started pacing the floor.

"I just put in a call to my connect, the Morettis. If they don't handle this Rossi fool, I'll do it my damn self," Real said sincerely.

"Bro, just get me this spic's location, and I'll eliminate all of this tough guy talk! Fuck them slick heads!" Cash shouted as he continued to pace the room.

"I'm going to see what the Morettis do first. There may be no need for us to bother. What's the word on the street?" Real asked, changing the subject.

"Everythang moving lovely. I had to chastise a lil' nigga this morning about an overdue debt, but all in all, everything moving like clockwork," Cash said as he sat back down in the office chair.

"Well, you know I got a shipment coming in this week, and it's mandatory that it go quicker than the last. Oh, by the way... I hear Deuce and them on the west side are putting down real heavy. What's up with that?" Real inquired.

"Yeah, word is they got a new Colombian connect out of Miami. My crew and I were just discussing that yesterday. We are working on eliminating that problem before the end of the week," Cash assured Real.

"A'ight. We don't need to be sitting on this shit no longer than a week," Real said firmly.

"I got you. I'm getting with my niggas tomorrow to handle that west side problem, and also I'll connect with my folks in New York and L.A. with some good numbers to make that shit disappear."

"A'ight. And about that west side problem, let them niggas on payroll handle it. Don't get your hands dirty. They expendable, and you ain't," Real said firmly, knowing all too well how Cash liked to get his hands dirty.

"I'm just calling the shots, bro. Let me know if you need me to handle that slick back," Cash said as he stood to leave.

"Get at me tomorrow."

"Fo sho," Cash replied as he exited.

En route home, Cash picked up his cell phone and called B-Low, not realizing that a black crown Victoria driven by a federal DEA agent followed close behind.

Chapter 4

" Ya'll niggas can't fuck with the Deuce!" Deuce screamed as he and a couple of his workers played *Madden* on the big screen in the back of D-Cuts, his neighborhood barbershop, which was really his drug distribution center.

It was two o'clock in the evening when four men dressed in all black with stockings over their faces entered Deuce's two-station barbershop on MLK. It was a slow day in the shop. One barber was cutting the hair of one of Deuce's crew members when the men rushed in. The last man, Big Trent, secured the door as B-Low, Jesse, and Pete pulled their weapons on the two men at the chair.

"Don't move, niggas!" Pete said firmly to the barber as he laid the Wahl clippers down on the counter.

"Both of ya'll niggas get in here!" Jesse screamed, holding the door to the utility closet open.

"Okay, homies, we don't want no problems," the man in the chair pleaded as Jesse secured them in the closet.

"Touch down!" Deuce screamed from the back of the shop, unaware of what was going on out front.

"Ah, nigga, you ain't did nothing. Get back!" one of Deuce's workers screamed.

Just as Deuce was resetting the game, the three men burst into the back room with guns drawn.

Jesse, the deadliest of the crew, was leading the pack. "Don't move, bitches!" Jesse screamed as he leveled his gun at the three men sitting on the leather couch.

"Whoa! Hold up, folks!" Deuce screamed with his hands in the air.

"All y'all get down! NOW!" B-Low screamed.

Just then, one of Deuce's workers went for his gun. The worker let off a wild shot in B-Low's direction that hit Pete in the side of his head, killing him instantly. Seeing Pete drop, Jesse and B-Low didn't waste time unloading their guns into Deuce and his workers. Trent, who stood guard at the door, rushed to the back of the shop after hearing the shots. Seeing his lil' brother Pete's head splattered sent him into a frenzy. Big Trent promptly unloaded his Glock 40 into the already dead men.

"Come on, man. Let's go!" Jesse screamed to Trent, who was sliding another clip in his gun.

"Let's go, bro!" B-Low screamed as they all took off running through the shop.

Just as Trent was about to exit the shop, he thought about his lil' brother Pete in the back of the shop, lying there lifeless. Then he thought about the men in the closet. He almost got left behind while he unloaded another clip into the cowering men in the closet. A few seconds later, he was jumping into the stolen minivan with Jesse and B-Low.

On the way back out to the south side, Jesse called Cash on his cell phone. "Shit taken care of," Jesse said in a sinister tone, still thinking about poor Pete, who didn't make it alive.

"Much appreciated. The money will be at the usual spot at six," Cash stated and ended the call.

Chapter 5

" *W*ake up! Wake up! Wake up!" Constance chanted as she brought the tray full of food upstairs to Real as he lay in bed.

"All this for me?" Real asked groggily, rolling over.

"Yep. So get on up," Constance demanded playfully.

"Well, yes, ma'am!" Real screamed jokingly.

Real lay in bed and ate breakfast while Constance got ready for a meeting with a very important client who was looking to purchase a $12 million dollar property out in the Buckhead area.

"Damn, somebody looking way to good just to be selling a house," Real called out, admiring Constance in her designer pant suit and high heels.

"A *$12 million* house! Get it right!" Constance shouted back playfully.

"Excuse me! Can't wait to see *that* commission check!"

"Whatever. What's up with the foreigners?" she asked, referring to the Italians.

"I should be getting a call back soon. If not, I'll just go see this Rossi dude myself."

"Just be careful, baby, please," Constance said softly as she walked over to him sitting on the side of the bed and hugged him tight.

"Everythang gonna be all good. Now go make that money," Real said, patting her on her plump ass as she walked off on her way to her meeting.

Five minutes after Constance pulled out of the driveway, Real's phone rang. Checking the screen, he saw it was old man Moretti.

"Hello," Real answered, already knowing who it was.

"Hi, my buddy. How are you?" Moretti asked with a slight wheeze in his voice.

"I'm just fine, but it seems as if someone has a problem with me working with you," Real said, taking a seat in his bedroom recliner.

"No! No problem! What make you think that is so?" Moretti questioned.

"I had a visit by some men last night that work for a man by the name of Rossi. They told me—"

Before Real could finish, Moretti spat heatedly, "Fucking no good bastard! I spare him no longer! He knows better than to step into my territory! I will kill the unscrupulous son of a bitch! Angelo! Angelo!" Moretti screamed for his nephew, the second in command. "Hold for a second, my friend."

"Yeah," Real murmured.

"Angelo, that bastard Rossi is at it again! Let all the families know that the truce is off! After you alert everyone, report back to me," Moretti barked. "Hello?" Moretti called out.

"I'm here," Real replied as he reclined back in the chair.

"Sorry about that. My apologies. You will have no more problems from him or his people. Also, your delivery should be arriving real soon. Make sure you contact me when it does."

"Will do, and the remaining balance will be deposited in the Chase account Monday. Have a good weekend."

"You do the same, my friend."

Just as Real was hanging up with Moretti, his phone rang again. "Yeah?" Real spat.

"Where you at, cuz?" Max asked in panic.

"What's wrong, Max?" Real shouted.

"Cuz, you got auditions, remember? You got ten girls down here waiting on you to see if they qualify for the club," Max declared.

"Damn! I totally forgot. I'm on the way," Real said. He jumped up out of the recliner and got dressed quickly.

One weekend out of the month, Real invited girls in to try out for a dancing job in the club. He had totally forgotten that he changed it this month to Thursday. Speeding down to the club in his Range Rover Sport, he looked at his watch. He was only twenty minutes late.

A few minutes later, he was pulling up into the club parking lot. He jumped out of the truck and rushed in the club.

"Hey, cuz! Man, they waiting for you," Max said, meeting him as he entered.

It was lunch hour in the club—a time when it was more socializing than dancing. Most of the girls were still getting paid for their conversation.

The G-Spot was Real's special project. He had built the club from the ground up. The G-Spot held two full bars, a private party room, a glassed-in VIP section, two custom black and gold pool tables, and some of the most expensive handcrafted leather furniture with gold accents available. The G-Spot was the most luxurious strip club in the state—and he wanted the most luxurious girls to dance there, so he auditioned them all himself.

Chapter 6

*R*eal rushed over to the half-dressed women that stood lined up in front of his office door. "Ladies, sorry for keeping you waiting. I'm Real, the owner, as some of you already know," Real said recognizing two of the girls as he walked by them and into his office.

Right after Real introduced himself, Max showed up with a clipboard and pen. After getting all the girls' names, he entered Real's office. A few minutes later, he came back out and told the first girl on the list to go in.

After spending over two hours interviewing and inspecting the women, it was time for Real to head out and check on the drop. He gave Max the list of girls that made the cut and then sent him to check on the liquor supply before he ducked back into his office and called Cash.

"Yo! Yo!" Cashed shouted into the phone.

"What up, bro? Did my mail get there?" Real asked, referring to the 120 kilos of cocaine that was set to arrive.

"Yeah, it got here," Cash replied, standing in the middle of the stash house looking at the blocks of pure, uncut cocaine stacked up in the corner.

"I'll be out there in a lil' while," Real said, promptly hanging up the phone with Cash and then calling Moretti to let him know everything was in order.

Just as Real was hanging up with Moretti and getting ready to go, a text came through his phone from Cash that read: 'West side eliminated'. Real smiled, knowing now his work would move a lot faster.

Real was interrupted as he did the math in his head on the profit he would make off this most recent shipment. "Who is it?" Real screamed as he cleared his desk, getting ready to leave.

"Cream."

"Come in."

Cream slowly stepped into Real's office and closed the door behind her. Cream was the only girl in the club that Real had to think twice about. Cream was beyond beautiful. Her smooth, flawless skin, jet black natural curly hair, and light green eyes had Real tempted. Cream's nice round ass, wide hips, big track star legs, flat stomach, and perfect perky C cups were almost impossible to resist. Her pearly white and pretty smile would light up any room. Constance was the only thing stopping him from having Cream as his.

"Hey, Real," Cream said softly.

"What's going on?" Real asked her as she walked over and stood bowlegged in front of his desk in her red rhinestone string bikini with matching top and three-inch heels.

"You are what's going on. I'm still trying to get me a blockbuster night," Cream said seductively. She didn't hear Constance enter behind her at first.

Constance crossed her arms and made it a point to clear her throat quite loudly.

"Oh, hey, Constance," Cream stuttered when she turned and saw Real's woman standing there.

"Don't 'hey' me, bitch!" Constance screamed as she rushed across the room and got directly into Cream's face. "Look here, you ten-dollar, broke-down-ass ho! If you approach mine again, I promise you I'm going to beat your mutt ass all around this mutha-fuckin' club! No more passes, bitch! Now get the fuck up out of here and let them thirsty niggas out there fondle your trick ass!" Constance barked, wishing Cream would get wrong.

Real sat back quietly and watched the exchange.

"It ain't even like—" Cream started.

"Bitch, get the fuck out of here!" Constance snapped.

Cream turned and hurried out of the office with her hooker heels click-clacking down the hall.

"Nigga, what you got that bitch all up here for with her shit hanging out everywhere?" Constance asked while walking around the desk and getting in Real's face.

"A'ight now. Sit down. You know better than to even think like that," Real said, snatching her down into his lap.

"I know you just ain't puttin' your hands on me," Constance said playfully.

"Yeah, I did so straighten your business," Real told her as he grabbed the back of her head and kissed her roughly.

Despite Cream's pathetic advances, Constance knew Real wouldn't ever betray her on any level. She knew they had a bond that could never be broken. Constance totally trusted Real. She counted the days to their wedding, which was set for the beginning of the upcoming year. Constance couldn't also wait for the day that their love child was conceived. She regularly found herself saying a silent prayer after their lovemaking for Real's child.

On the flipside, Real knew he had a woman above the rest—a woman that couldn't be anything other than loyal, devoted, and 100 percent down with her man. She was his Bonnie, and he was her Clyde.

"What brings you to these parts of town?" Real asked Constance, rubbing her thighs.

"I was in the neighborhood. My meeting was right down the street in the new office plaza off of Third Street," Constance said, rubbing her long red manicured nails along his neck.

"How did everything go?" Real asked, feeling an erection

coming on.

"Everything went great. We closing on it Tuesday," Constance replied. She could feel his hard-on.

"That's my girl. I taught you well," Real joked.

"Yeah, whatever. Get your dick off my leg, freak," Constance said playfully.

"Can't help it," Real replied, reaching around and pulling her all the way into his lap.

"Well, it's time for me to go," Constance joked, leaning to get up off Real's lap.

"You lucky I got business to handle, or else I'd fuck the shit out of you right here and now," Real declared, letting her up.

"Yeah, I am lucky—especially if you were going to fuck the shit out of me! Damn!" Constance laughed as she headed to the door.

"Love you, girl," Real said as Constance opened the door to leave.

"Love you, boy," Constance replied as she exited.

"Say, fella, can I get a Coke, light on the ice," the federal agent asked the bartender as he watched Constance walk by him, leaving the club.

A few minutes later, Real exited his office and told Max he would get with him tomorrow. The young agent sat his glass down and followed as Real made his way to the parking lot.

Chapter 7

$\mathscr{C}$onstance turned left out of the club parking lot and headed home while Real made a right en route to the stash house. A while back, Real had purchased the small two-bedroom brick house that was located off Fairburn Road in a quiet neighborhood. Real and Cash were the only ones who knew about the house and its location.

Every time a shipment came in, they would meet at the house to make sure everything was accounted for. Real made it his business to count every block of cocaine sent to him. After the product was inventoried, Real would contact Moretti to confirm everything, and Cash would take it to the streets for distribution.

As Real turned onto the street that led to the stash house, he noticed a black official-looking car behind him. Playing it safe, just in case, Real made a quick detour and headed out to Greenbriar Mall. The black car continued straight as Real turned into the mall parking lot. One thing Real always practiced was playing it safe at all times, and he always followed his first intuition. Thus far, it had kept him and his business alive.

After cruising the mall parking lot, Real determined that everything was clear. Five minutes later, he was pulling into the stash house carport.

"What's up, bro? Would have been here sooner, but a black

car looked like it was following me. It was a false alarm. I still had to bust a block to make sure. What's good?" Real said as he closed the carport entrance door behind him.

"Everything accounted for—120 all wrapped up like presents on Christmas morning," Cash said as he entered the room that contained the cocaine.

"I wonder why it's red this time?" Real asked, looking at the red tape the shipment was wrapped in.

"Probably ran out of gray and black," Cash said, walking over and inspecting one of the wrapped up kilos.

After making sure everything added up, Real called Moretti again to confirm the correct count. After all confirmations, Real and Cash both vigorously dialed numbers into their cell phones. They were so busy with their biz that they did not notice the black Crown Vic cruising by the house.

Thirty minutes later, they were pulling out of the driveway. Real was en route home, and Cash was on the way to meet his east side connect with twenty kilos.

Cash cruised east on 285 in his beat up old Chrysler LeBaron work car, heading out to Decatur to meet with Thad and Reg, two brothers that had most of the east side on lock. Cash didn't notice the black Crown Vic three cars behind. After following Cash for a short distance, the man behind the wheel picked up his cell phone and called the other unmarked car up ahead. After a brief conversation, that man decided to dispatch a Georgia state trooper, and a few minutes later, the trooper was pulling into the lane behind Cash.

"Shit!" Cash spat as the trooper turned on his lights, motioning for Cash to pull over. Having no other choice, Cash slowly pulled over into the emergency lane. Just as he was putting the car in park, the black Crown Vic pulled up behind the state trooper. "Fuck!" Cash screamed as he threw open the car door and made a mad dash for the woods.

"Freeze!" the state trooper yelled as Cash continued running ignoring his orders. The two federal agents took off behind Cash, catching him before he made it into the woods.

"Don't fuckin' move!" the young White federal agent screamed as he grinded his knee into Cash's back.

"Ya'll got it!" Cash screamed out in pain as they roughly handcuffed him.

Searching the car, they found the twenty kilos of cocaine, an unregistered handgun, an ounce of weed, and twelve ecstasy pills. They placed Cash into the back of the unmarked car, the fed thanked the state trooper, and then hauled Cash down to the federal holding facility.

Chapter 8

*A*fter handling business all day, Real decided it was time to give Constance some quality time. On the way home, Real stopped by the local florist and picked up a dozen red roses.

"Oh, baby!" Constance screamed, placing her hands over her mouth as Real walked in the house holding the flowers.

"For my special lady," Real said as he handed Constance the fresh roses.

"Thank you, baby! Love you," Constance called out.

"Love you too," Real replied as he leaned around the roses and gently kissed Constance on the neck.

"Ooh! Alright now," Constance said faintly.

"Alright what?" Real said playfully.

"You win for now. Dinner will be ready in a minute."

"That'll work. I'm going to grab a quick shower," Real said as he turned and headed up to the bedroom.

Constance prepared Real's favorite: grilled chicken breast, buttered rolls, potatoes, green beans, and a glass of white wine. Constance called Real down to the dining room table that they rarely used as she poured his wine in his glass.

"What's up with all the special attention tonight?" Constance inquired as Real sat down and started eating.

"You know, sometimes a man got to show his woman how

much she is loved and appreciated," Real answered, devouring his favorite meal.

"Oh, for real, Real!" Constance joked as she poked at a green bean, moving it around on the plate with her fork.

"Yeah for real!" Real shot back laughing.

After finishing off dinner, they retired to the bedroom. While Constance took her shower, Real flipped the channels back and forth between ESPN and BET.

As Constance stepped out of the bathroom, she grabbed her silk robe from the chair and put it on, neglecting to tie it up. After all the time they had been together, Real was still mesmerized by Constance's perfect body and beautiful features. Constance walked over to the bed and slid in next to Real.

"Hey, get your wet self off me," Real joked, sliding away from her.

"Boy, shut up and get over here," Constance barked as she quickly removed her robe and climbed on top of him. Real wiggled out of his boxers as Constance kissed on his chest.

Feeling his dick grow hard, Constance slowly reached back and stroked it. When it was hard as a brick, she leaned up and slowly guided it into her waiting, dripping wet pussy. "Ohh shiiit!" Constance moaned as she grinded up and down on Real's dick.

"Yeah baby! Yeah!" Real uttered as Constance looked into his eyes and rode him slowly.

Picking up the pace, Real had Constance screaming for more. Real gripped her ass and spread it as he raised up off the bed, meeting her every stroke.

"Oh, give it to me, Daddy! Oh shit, baby!" Constance screamed, digging her nails into his chest.

Slowing down the pace, Real pulled out, flipped her around, and positioned Constance on her knees. He grabbed her ass and lifted her cheeks and then slid in slowly.

Constance held onto the headboard as Real pounded her roughly from behind. "Oh yes! Don't stop! Fuck this pussy!"

Constance screamed passionately as she looked back at him.

"Hell, yeah! Ah, shit! YES!" Real shouted, grabbing her by the hips and pulling her to him, making her challenge every stroke. Real buried his dick deep inside of Constance's wet pussy time and time again.

"Baby I'm...I'm...I...I'm about to...Oh shit, I'm cumming!" Constance screamed as her whole body shook and shivered.

After Constance spewed all of her body fluids all over Real's dick, Real laid Constance down on her back and climbed between her legs. Pinning her legs back as far as they would go, he wasted no time sticking his hard dick back into Constance's warm center.

"Oooh! Ah, damn!" Constance screamed as Real proceeded to reach his climax.

"Damn, baby! Oh yeah! Right there, boo! Ah! Ah! It's coming, baby! Yeahhh!" Real moaned as Constance locked her legs around his back. She smiled and held him tight as he filled her with his juices.

They were much too busy in the heat of their passion to notice the federal agent outside of the house snapping pictures.

Chapter 9

The next morning, Cash was curled up on the cold steel bench when the hulking federal agent entered the room

"Corey Fields, let's go!" the federal agent yelled, startling Cash out of his sleep.

"I need to call my lawyer," Cash uttered as he rolled over, placing his feet flat on the cold cement floor.

"Yeah, I've heard it before, but right now you're coming with me," the agent said firmly.

Cash didn't resist as he followed the sunburned agent down the hall into a conference room where two other agents dressed in suits and ties sat at a table covered with files.

"Take a seat," the hulking agent said, pointing to the small wooden chair at the table with the other agents.

"Corey Fields…my man! What up, brother?" the middle-aged, overweight Black agent called out as Cash took a seat at the table.

"Naw man, that's Cash!" the young White agent sitting behind the table called out.

Cash sat at the table, staring at the two men, not saying a word.

"Mr. Cash let's—"

"I need to call my lawyer," Cash demanded, cutting the agent off.

"Okay, Mr. Fields, but first I think you should hear us out. Oh, by the way, I'm Agent Ross, this is Agent Kincaide, and your escort is Agent Spencer. Kincaide and I are assigned to your file," the overweight Ross said.

"Yeah, we've been checking you out for a minute, Cash. Really, all in all, you're not the one we're hunting. We need your boss, Richard Walker, aka the infamous Real," Kincaide said and then paused to see how Cash would react.

"I don't know no 'Real' or 'Richard'. I need to call my lawyer," Cash insisted.

"Oh you know him alright," Agent Ross spat while pulling a stack of photos out of the folders scattered out over the table.

"Can't say I do," Cash said with sarcasm.

"Who the fuck is this then?" Ross asked, sliding the pictures down to Cash.

They had pictures of him and Real in Vegas at the MGM Grand, some of them at the BET Awards in Atlanta, a couple of them at the stash house, and some of them at the club. They even had pictures of Real and Constance lounging out in their back yard by the pool.

"Now let me ask you again. Do you know Richard Walker?" Agent Kincaide asked, reaching to take the photos back.

"Nope," Cash said, sticking to his lie.

"Well, let's put it like this. We talked to the prosecutor this morning before Agent Spencer came and got you. She's looking to lock you away for over 100 years. Now, you and I know you wouldn't live that long, but before we left her office we made a deal with her. The only way she'll agree to our deal is if you cooperate 100 percent. She's willing to sweep your charges under the rug, but only if you help us bring down Richard Walker," Ross said as an eerie quietness settled over the room.

"Help you? Man, I told you, I don't know no Richard or Real. Ya'll get me a phone so I can call my lawyer. I ain't got shit to say!" Cash snapped as he sat upright in the small wooden chair.

"Look here, Cash, you're going to help us, or we are going to make sure you never walk a free man again. We got twenty kilos, weed, a gun, and all kinds of illegal shit—enough for us to bury your ass," Agent Kincaide said forcefully.

"I don't know what you're talking about," Cash quivered.

Seeing Cash about to give in, Ross spoke. "Look, Cash we can really help you, but you got to help us. You help us bring down Richard Walker, and the prosecutor will agree to drop your charges and hide you out in the witness protection program. Richard is a smart man. He's evaded us completely, not giving us anything solid for some time now, but with you, we can change all that. Cash if you decide not to help us, we will just run you to trial for the twenty kilos and all the other stuff we found. There's no doubt we will find you guilty and let you rot away in prison. You'll be sharing bunks with some con who wants to make you his boyfriend while Richard is still out living the good life," Ross said firmly.

"Man…" Cash said, thinking about the twenty kilos and solid evidence against him. He knew he would most definitely lose in trial. Cash dropped his head and thought about everything. He was totally against snitching and being an informant, but now, being in this situation had him thinking twice. He knew it was his life or the man's that saved it. After a few minutes, Cash lifted his head and looked at both the federal agents. "What do I got to do?" he asked softly, dropping his head back down.

"This is what we need you to do…" Agent Ross began, looking over at Agent Kincaide with an accomplished, satisfied grin.

Chapter 10

The next morning, Constance left Real in bed as she hurried out of the house to meet with a potential buyer for one of her prime properties. "This house is one of my favorites. It's only two years old and practically unlived in," Constance told the tall, lanky, expensively dressed Italian man as they walked through the $1.7 million mansion in Fayetteville.

"Nice. Are there any golf courses nearby?" the man asked, waiting for the right time to make his move.

"Yeah. There're some real nice courses just ten minutes up the road," Constance told him. In the midst of their conversation, she had not heard another man enter the house from downstairs.

The potential client looked at his watch and saw that it was time. "Well, everything looks nice. What's in there?" he asked, pointing to a closed door.

Constance stepped in front of him to open the upstairs wine cellar door. "This? Oh, well, this is a—" The blow from behind cut Constance off mid sentence, knocking her out cold.

After checking to make sure Constance was out, the Italian ran down the stairs two at a time with his long, lanky legs and motioned for the other man to come upstairs.

"Where is she?" the heavyset Italian asked in a thick accent as they climbed the steps.

"In that room, out cold. I'll open the garage and pull the car in. We can take her out that way," the tall man said as he pointed the fat man to the room where Constance was. He then turned and hurried off to pull the car in the garage.

The big Italian tied Constance up and carried her down to the garage, where his partner waited in the old beat-up burgundy Delta 88. They secured her in the back seat and sped off.

"Uncle Rossi is not going to like this," the fat Italian said as they rode through downtown, en route to the old abandoned warehouse that they occasionally used as a hangout.

"Look, Saul, Uncle Rossi is getting soft and weak in his old age. He is letting this young punk Moretti push him around. I remember a time when Uncle Rossi would have sent him swimming with the fishes. Saul, we got to stand for the family honor," Milo explained.

"Milo, we are clearly going against Uncle Rossi and the other families. Eliminating this Real character might get us killed. I think we should rethink this," Saul said as he navigated the Delta 88 down the one-way street that led to the abandoned warehouse.

"Look, Saul, like I said, we have to save the family. This man Real is making Moretti stronger, and if we just sit around and let him get stronger and stronger, he will start controlling the cartel. He'll eventually put us all out of business," Milo explained as he peeped back at Constance, who was starting to come to.

"We will have to make it look like he has other enemies, and this has to be done really quickly. Moretti has reached out to other families, and they stand firm against Uncle Rossi's actions. They also made it clear that if Uncle eliminates Moretti's runner Real, they would strike out against us in every way. What we are doing now could clearly get uncle Rossi killed, so this has got to be done discreetly," Milo continued explaining as Saul pulled the car up to the warehouse entrance.

"I hope you're sure about all this," Saul mumbled as he got out and opened the back door of the car.

The old warehouse was hidden between other old buildings that the big corporations had abandoned years ago when automation put the need for big factories out of business. Just as Saul reached in to grab Constance, she woke up.

"What's going on? Where the fuck am I?" Constance screamed, still dazed as she tried to wiggle free from the cord wrapped around her wrists and ankles.

"Hey, just calm down, and everything will be okay," Saul said faintly.

"Why are you doing this?" Constance yelled as the tall, lanky Milo walked over to the back door of the car. Looking up at Milo, it hit her all at once. *That's the Italian from the club!*

"We have to send your man Real a message," Milo barked as he snatched Constance out of the car and carried her into the warehouse kicking and screaming.

Up until the cartel grew weak and things slowed down for them, Milo and his cousin Saul had used the abandoned warehouse as a drug distribution center, but now it was just their hangout. Looking at the drab warehouse from the outside, you would never know it was modestly furnished, including a full bathroom.

Milo and Saul were entertained by hookers at the warehouse from time to time. The warehouse had no windows and only one working exit. Bearing this in mind, the men knew this would be a good place to hold Constance hostage. They planned to use her as bait to draw Real out so they could do away with him.

"You just do as we say, and you will be okay, but if you go against our wishes, you will be killed," Milo said in a menacing tone as he pushed Constance into a dimly lit room with an old steel chair and a mildewed old stained mattress in the middle of the floor.

Constance pleaded with him as he closed the door and locked it. She knew these men were out to get rid of Real. She thought Real's friend Moretti had handled this problem, but obviously he hadn't, and as she realized this, she could do nothing but take a seat on the cold steel chair and cry.

Chapter 11

*A*s Cash exited the federal building, he stared at the official-looking business card Agent Kincaide had given him. The card had Agent Kincaide's number displayed under a government seal and Agent Ross's number scribbled on the back.

"Bullshit," Cash cursed under his breath as he looked for his car in the area Ross said it was parked. Spotting his car, he hurried over, trying his best not to be seen coming out of the federal building. As he opened the car door and got in, he noticed that everything was still in place. The twenty kilos were still in the duffle bag on the back seat, and his gun was still in the glove compartment, along with his weed and ecstasy pills.

The DA had agreed to work with Cash if he worked with her office in bringing down the multi-city drug operation that they knew—but hadn't yet been able to prove—Real was running. Part of the deal consisted of Cash wearing a wire and turning over all information he had on Real and his illegal activities. By the time Cash left the federal building, Ross and Kincaide had added two more full file folders to what they knew about Real.

As Cash pulled out of the federal building parking lot, his phone began to ring from where it was still positioned on the passenger's seat, right where he had tossed it when he made a run for it. "Yeah?" Cash answered, not recognizing the phone number displayed on the screen.

"Say, playa, what happened to you yesterday?' Reg, the dealer from Decatur, asked.

· "Oh damn, bro, my bad. Shit got real crazy around my way yesterday, but I ain't forgot about you. I got your pack in the back seat right now. Give me about an hour," Cash told Reg while looking down at his wrinkled clothes he was still wearing from the day before.

"A'ight. Just waiting on you," Reg replied and hung up.

Cash did a quick detour to his house to grab a shower and a change of clothes. As he pulled up at his half-a-million-dollar home, he noticed a white van in the driveway. He pulled up beside the van and focused in on the White man with shades on sitting behind the wheel. Cash jumped out of the car and aggressively approached the van, pistol in hand. "Who the fuck are you?" Cash screamed, pointing the pistol at the van driver.

"You can put that gun away, Mr. Fields. I'm Agent Trevor Blakely. I'll be monitoring your wire. I've been waiting on you to show up so I could run a test and activate the wire."

"What? They said I would only have to wear the wire when a deal goes down! Why the hell you out here at my house and shit?" Cash screamed as he tucked his gun in his waistband.

"Look, Mr. Fields, you agreed and signed papers. Don't forget that we still can pin you with that stuff you're riding around with in your car!" the agent snapped.

"Fuck this shit, man! This wasn't the fucking deal!" Cash yelled, looking around rubbing his head.

"Okay, fine. I'll just call Ross and let him know you've changed your mind and that the deal is off," the agent said calmly as he leaned back in his seat and pulled his cell phone from his pocket.

"Look here, man…I ain't got no problem wearing no wire, but ya'll don't need to be all at my house and shit!" Cash screamed, hating the position he was in.

Without replying, the man reached over and pushed open the door so Cash could get in. Cash reluctantly climbed in and took notes on how the wire worked. They placed it under his shirt and did a test run. Cash was totally uncomfortable wearing the wire. All he could think about was if he was ever caught wearing it and how his life would end. After going over the procedures for the third time, Cash had it down pat and regretted every minute of it. Seeing that everything was in line, the agent commended Cash on his cooperation and patted him on the back as Cash opened up the van door and got out.

Cash wasn't used to this part of the game, and he hated it. He was now forced to bring down a man that was like a brother to him. Backing out of the deal was not an option; he loved Real, but he loved his freedom more.

As Cash stood under the warm shower, he thought about the situation he was in and closed his eyes when the water tumbled down over his head. Ten minutes later, he was leaving the house on the way out to Decatur to meet with Reg and Thad.

He exited at Glenwood and turned right and then made another quick right. Cash peered up at the Old English Inn, where Reg and Thad had set up shop. He made a left up into the inn parking lot and took in the scene. The walking zombies who were once productive citizens were out full blast, on the prowl for drugs. The Old English was home to the black sheep of society, the people who just so happened to keep Cash and Real in business.

As Cash pulled around to the back of the inn, he saw Thad sitting out on his SUV with a group of young dealers. He pulled up beside them. "What up, nigga?" Cash screamed as he opened his car door and got out.

"What it is, playboy?" Thad fired back as he jumped off of his Denali and gave Cash five.

As they greeted each other, Cash couldn't help thinking about the wire taped to his chest.

"Everything good?" Where that boy Reg at?" Cash asked,

looking around and keeping an eye on the group of young hustlers. Cash didn't trust nobody.

"That nigga up in the spot waiting on you," Thad said, nodding in the direction of the room.

"A'ight. Come on so we can handle this biz. I got thangs to do," Cash said firmly, still watching the group of young hustlers as he reached in the car and grabbed the duffle bag off the back seat.

"No doubt," Thad replied as he led the way up to the room.

Reg was entertaining a thick red bone when Cash and Thad entered. "What up, man?" Reg said with enthusiasm as Thad and Cash walked through the door of the shabbily furnished room.

"What it is, fam?" Cash replied, walking over to the small wooden table.

"Say, go get yourself something to eat," Reg instructed the red bone as he threw her keys. Reading between the lines, she asked no questions before she hurried out of the door.

"What we got here?" Reg asked as Cash emptied the contents of the bag on the table.

"Twenty blocks, all weighed up. Our tag is eighteen-five a piece, so we looking at three hundred seventy grand," Cash uttered, thinking about the wire taped to his chest.

"Hold up now, bro. You said this drop was going to be a flat eighteen a piece, remember?" Thad said as he walked over to the table.

"Boy, you dead right, I forgot. Eighteen even, so that's um…. three sixty straight up and down," Cash agreed.

"Good deal. Here you go. It is all counted, down to the penny," Reg said as he handed Cash the backpack full of money that he retrieved from under the bed.

"Check dat!" Cash said, not wasting time counting the money. He had been dealing with the brothers for years and knew their money was good. He slapped the brothers five, threw the bag over his shoulder, and exited the room.

Stepping out the door, he saw the young dealers huddled up

in a circle shooting dice. Watching everything that moved, Cash hurried over to his car with the bag of money. He cranked up the LeBaron and dropped it in drive before he sped out of the Old English Inn on his way to the G-Spot.

The black Crown Vic waited until Cash was out of the parking lot to make its move. "All units standby. I repeat...all units standby," the agent barked into the radio as they got into position to storm the room where Reg and Thad were with the twenty kilos.

" *S*ay, Max, you need to start letting me know beforehand when the bar stock gets low. Now we got to water shit down just to get through the weekend," Real said firmly while sitting behind his desk writing up an order for more liquor.

"My bad cuz, man, that nigga Del ain't even say nothing. He back there making all them dranks and ain't even holla at me," Max said, wiping the sweat from his face.

"It's your job to be on top of all that, Max! You got to lighten up seriously. This is the last time," Real told Max as he continued filling out the liquor purchase order.

"It won't happen again, cuz. I promise you that," Max said proudly with a pitiful look on his face.

While Max and Real were in the back office talking, Cash was walking through the club front door with the backpack full of money slung over his shoulder. Most of the girls knew Cash, being that he paid a lot of them for sex. He walked through the club looking for new meat. Checking out the black as charcoal Jaguar up on stage and not paying attention to where he was going, he just so happened to bump into Cream.

"Excuse you!" Cream screamed over the Young Jeezy blasting out of the club speakers.

"Aw, my bad, Cream. What up?" Cash said, looking her up

and down.

"Ain't nothing up!" Cream replied forcefully, letting him know she was still not one to be bought.

Cash had propositioned Cream her first night at the club. Taken in by how bad Cream was, he offered her double his normal price of $500. She snapped and cursed him out, and ever since that day, the two had been at constant odds.

"Damn! It's like that?" Cash asked, watching Cream's backside jiggle out of control as she walked off.

After checking Jaguar out one more time, Cash hurried off to Real's office. "Knock! Knock!"

"Yeah?" Real yelled as Max turned toward the door.

"Me!" Cash screamed.

"Come in!" Real replied.

Max took Cash's entrance as his cue to leave.

"What up, Max?" Cash said as Max shot by him.

"What's up, Cash?" Max replied as he hurried out the door back to the club floor.

"What's this?" Real asked. He knew it was money, though he had no idea how much.

"Three hundred sixty grand," Cash said. He swallowed hard as he dropped the backpack on Real's desk, still thinking about the wire taped to his chest.

"Bro, like I told you, this drop got to go way faster than the last one. That's the only way I'll be able to get Moretti down on the price," Real explained as he pulled the bag over to him.

"I got you. I got half of it already spoken for. I'm on my way out of Union City now. All this shit will be gone by Thursday guaranteed," Cash assured Real, still thinking about the feds who were listening in.

"A'ight, bro. If they gone by then, I'll put in for one fifty more, but this time, our tag will be ten flat," Real said with enthusiasm.

"That's love! I'm on it. And, oh, by the way—"

Beep! Beep! Beep!

Real's beeping cell phone cut Cash off. "Hey, baby," Real answered, seeing Constance's number and picture flash across the screen.

"Hey, my friend. Listen and listen good. If you want to see your beautiful lady again, you need to deliver $250,000 to the Druid Hills golf course at eight o'clock sharp tonight. You need to be by yourself. Any funny business, and your lady friend here will never be seen alive again," Milo said in a menacing tone as he stood in the doorway of the room where Constance was kept.

Real wasn't sure whether to believe the call or not—his heart skipped a beat when he heard Constance crying loudly in the background.

Chapter 13

" *As* long as your man Real cooperates, everything will work just fine," Milo said as he slammed the door to the room that housed Constance and slid her cell phone into his back pocket.

Milo and Saul sat on the couch and went over the night's plan while loading their weapons. Milo's money demands were just a ploy to make Real think their motive was money. Their true motive was taking his life.

Milo's plan to take over the family was falling into place quite smoothly. Milo's true intentions were to get his Uncle Rossi eliminated. He planned to make Real's murder look like it was ordered by Mr. Rossi himself, and in turn, he knew the other families would wage war and ultimately kill Rossi for going against the family truce. Since Milo was second in charge, he would be placed at the head of the family with Rossi's demise. Milo also knew Saul was a smart man and in due time would figure out his plans, so he'd have to eliminate his cousin right along with all of the others. He wanted to take his rightful place as head—and at all costs.

"You got everything mapped out right? You know this has to look like it came from bad dealings and not us, right?" Saul asked as he loaded the buck shots into the twelve-gauge shotgun.

"I got everything worked out. You know I would never be so

reckless. Go get the girl and tie her back up," Milo said, cocking his chrome nine-millimeter, holding it up and admiring it.

Milo had everything planned out. The golf course would surely be deserted when they arrived. It was the perfect spot, being that it was in a secluded location in the middle of nowhere. Milo planned to get Saul to escort Constance to Real and exchange her for the money. Just as the exchange was going down, he would unload his gun on all of them, leaving no one alive.

"You haven't told anyone of our plans, have you?" Milo asked Saul as he returned to the room after tying Constance up.

"No. No one."

Milo had been waiting for this day for the longest time. He was now going to be appointed head of the family. Milo was fed up with his uncle's passive ways. As far as he was concerned, Mr. Rossi had become weak and feeble and was merely a liability in his old age. Milo desperately needed to get the respect of the family back, even if it meant getting his uncle killed, which would surely happen when the other families suspected Rossi went against their word and had Real killed. Going against the families was a mandatory death sentence.

"It's almost time to load up," Milo said, looking at his watch and tucking the nine in the back of his pants.

Saul went to the back room and retrieved Constance, who was lying on the stained mattress with her ankles and wrists tied. "Time to go," Saul said as he entered the room and walked over to pick her up.

"Please," she begged. "If it's money you want, I will give it to you," Constance pleaded as Saul easily picked her up and heaved her over his shoulder.

"If your friend cooperates, you will be free to go. We are going to meet him now," Saul said as he carried her through the warehouse and out to the car.

Saul placed Constance in the back seat and then returned to the warehouse to get his guns.

"You ready?' Everything loaded up?" Milo asked Saul, grabbing his nine-millimeter from his back to check it again before he replaced it.

"The girl is already in the car. I'm getting the guns now," Saul replied as he grabbed the twelve-gauge shotgun and thirty-eight revolver off the couch.

"Let's ride," Milo said, looking at his watch. It was seven thirty.

Riding through downtown on the way to meet Real, Milo thought about the changes he would make when he was place in control of the family. He planned to wage war on anyone that got in his way. He was determined to bring the power back to the family. He hated to have to kill Saul, but Saul was his calling card that would tip everyone off that Rossi had ordered the hit. The families would all come together and talk about how Saul, Mr. Rossi's nephew and known hit man, was found dead with Real, the man Rossi was told by the family not to mess with. As soon as the family meeting was over, the decision to kill Mr. Rossi would be made, and after his death, Milo would be appointed.

Milo smiled at the thought as he navigated the Delta 88 through downtown.

Chapter 14

*A*fter Milo hung up the phone, Real went into a rage, slamming his cell phone against the wall. Cash jumped, startled by Real's reaction.

"Whoa! What up, bro?" Cash called out as Real lost his cool, which he seldom did.

"Constance has been snatched up!" Real screamed as he paced the floor.

After a few minutes of ranting, Real filled Cash in on the conversation.

"Who do you think it is, bro?" Cash asked, rubbing his chin in thought.

"Man, I have no idea! The mutha fucker sounded Spanish… maybe Italian. Fuck, man, I don't know!" Real spat as he paced the room.

"You think it could be the business with the slick heads that came in the club the other night?" Cash asked.

"Naw. Moretti gave me his word that he was going to handle that, and then he hit me back later and told me everything was taken care of. One thang about them Italians is they live by a code of honor, so really, that rules this Rossi dude out. Bro, I swear, somebody is going to die behind this bullshit!" Real snapped as he stood up behind his desk.

Agent Blakely took notes as Real waged murder on the kid-nappers.

"Man, let's just get these fools the money and get Constance back. We can deal with their sorry asses after that!" Cash snapped, disregarding the man listening in.

"Get with your people and get them down here ASAP!" Real barked, grabbing the bag of money and opening it.

"I'm on it," Cash said as he pulled out his cell phone and called B-Low and Jesse.

After listening in on Real and Cash, Agent Blakely called Agent Ross and filled him in on the kidnapping. Before they hung up the phone, Agent Ross was dispatching two undercover agents out to the golf course.

"Bro, we got to play this shit to the tee. I don't want nothing to happen to Constance," Real said as he counted out the $250,000 and put it in the backpack.

"I know, bro. B-Low and Jesse will be here in a minute. They are going to tail you out there. They'll be all the way out of sight," Cash said, toning it down for the listening agent.

"A'ight, I'm going to vest up just in case," Real said as he walked over to the office closet and grabbed his Kevlar vest.

After making plans with Real, Cash went out front to wait on B-Low and Jesse. Five minutes later, they were pulling up in an old green Chevy.

"What it do?" Cash said as he slapped five with B-Low and Jesse as they got out of the car.

"You tell me. What's the move?" B-Low asked as Jesse listened in on the plans.

"This is what's happening. My man's old lady been snatched up. The kidnappers want him to bring 250 grand to get her back. They are meeting him tonight at eight at the Druid Hills golf course. I want ya'll to trail him and watch his back, but you got to stay out of sight," Cash explained in a passive way because of the wire. He really wanted to order the men to murder the kidnappers on sight, but he thought better of it.

"Okay, so you just want us to stay hid but at the same time watch your people back?" Jesse asked, listening to the unusual request coming from Cash.

"Yeah. Just watch his back," Cash said, biting his tongue.

Jesse and B-Low sat in the car while Cash went back in the club to let Real know everything was in place. "Everything good, bro. I'll be laying back. B-Low and Jesse know what to do," Cash assured Real as they walked out of the office.

Real wasted no time getting into the Range Rover and heading out to the golf course. As he navigated through traffic he pulled open the glove box and made sure his Glock 40 was there. Glancing back in his rearview mirror, he saw B-Low and Jesse dipped low in the seat of the old Chevy, following him from a distance.

Agent Ross was on the phone with the two dispatched agents as they zeroed in on Milo and Saul pulling into the golf course parking lot. Ross had to make a critical decision in interfering with the kidnapping. He knew interference could blow their cover, but at the same time, he couldn't sit back and watch someone get murdered. Thinking fast, Ross radioed a uniformed officer and gave him instructions to pull the kidnappers over for a traffic violation and then arrest them. Ross crossed his fingers, hoping their cover wouldn't be blown. The investigation was days from being over, and Real would be out of business for good.

Chapter 15

The rookie officer spotted the Delta 88 sitting in the far corner of the golf course parking lot. Since they were not en route, he couldn't cite them for a moving violation, so he decided on the next best thing: loitering on private property.

As he neared the golf course entrance, he made out two men sitting in the front seat of the vehicle. Pulling his cruiser into the parking lot, he rounded the building and pulled up directly behind the Delta 88 and hit his blue lights.

"Shit!" Milo screamed as the officer's blue lights sent an eerie glow over the parking lot.

"Man, that fucker called the police!" Saul shouted as he watched the police cruiser through the rearview mirror.

Constance was relieved, but scared that the men may turn their guns on her. She couldn't believe Real had called the police. *That's not his style,* she thought. *My man handles his own shit.*

"Just be cool," Milo said as he pulled his nine from the small of his back and gripped it tightly in his hand.

The young, White, tobacco-chewing officer got out of his cruiser and approached the car. The two undercover federal agents sat a quarter mile down the road, watching the interaction through high-powered binoculars. The rookie officer walked up to the driver's side window and tapped it, telling Milo to let the window down. Just as Milo got the window halfway down, the officer noticed Constance tied up in the back seat. The officer's eyes grew as big as golf balls as he reached for his gun, but it was too late. Milo had leveled the nine-millimeter and pulled the trigger. The bullets ripped through the young rookie's nice creased uniform and entered his chest, knocking him off his feet. Constance screamed at the sight of the young officer being blown away.

"Damn it, Milo!" Saul screamed as Milo turned the ignition and snatched the car in gear.

Before they could clear the parking lot, the two federal agents were in full swing after watching the young rookie get killed. They radioed for backup as they positioned their car to block the entrance.

"Fuck…man!" Milo screamed as they saw the car blocking the entrance.

Mashing the gas on the Deltal 88, Milo barreled straight for the agents' car that was blocking their way out. The federal agents took aim at the oncoming vehicle. As the car charged them, they let off shot after shot. Milo and Saul crouched down into the seat and braced themselves as the Delta 88 clipped the rear end of the federal vehicle and sped out of the parking lot. Constance was being thrown around the back seat like a ragdoll.

Just as Milo and Saul cleared the parking lot, three police cruisers were rounding the curb, coming right in their direction. The two federal agents jumped into their car, which was mashed up in the rear, and gave chase also.

Seeing cruisers coming from behind and up ahead, Milo knew he was at odds. Pushing the Delta 88 to its top speed, he jumped the curb and took the car down an embankment that ran along a heavily wooded area.

"Man, we can't dodge 'em. They everywhere!" Saul screamed as he tightened his grip on his thirty-eight.

"Fuck! Fuck! Fuck!" Milo screamed as he wheeled the car as

close as he could to the wooded area.

The police were hot on their tail as they left the street and headed down the embankment. Milo saw an opening in the heavily wooded area and slammed on the brakes. Before the car came to a complete stop, Milo was jumping out. Following Milo's lead, Saul fumbled with the door as the police closed in. The police were hot on his tail as he finally got the door open and jumped out. Saul bolted from the car with the revolver still in his tight grip as he ran for the woods.

"Freeze!" the old White veteran officer yelled as he took aim at Saul.

Saul continued to sprint toward the woods, ignoring the officer's order. Just as Saul got a good stride going, the officer opened fire, hitting him in the back three times and knocking him face first to the ground. One officer secured Saul as the others continued after Milo. Constance was dazed when the two officers untied her and pulled her from the back of the Delta 88.

Milo continued to run hard, not looking back. He came up on a residential neighborhood after clearing the woods. When he did finally look back, he saw no signs of the uniformed officers. Coming out of the woods and trying not to look suspicious, Milo walked briskly through the neighborhood. A few minutes later, he was breaking into a car and stealing it for his long ride back home.

The uniformed officers lost sight of Milo in the darkness, so they doubled back and got the dogs. After combing the woods with the dogs, they concluded that the other man had gotten away. A few minutes later, they were focusing back on Saul, who was laid out on the wet grass. The EMT arrived minutes later, but it was too late. Saul coughed hard one last time before he took his last breath.

Chapter 16

eal pushed the Range Rover down the interstate, exceeding the speed limit on his way to the golf course. B-Low and Jesse bobbed their heads to the Scarface playing from the Chevy's two-knob cassette player as they pushed the Chevy to the limit, trying to keep up with Real in the Range.

All Real could think about was Constance. He prayed the men didn't hurt her. Two hundred and fifty thousand was a small price to pay for his soul mate. Racking his brain still trying to figure out who was behind the kidnapping, Real grabbed his cell phone from the console and dialed Moretti's number.

"Hi, Real. How's it going? You ready so soon?" Moretti asked, sure Real was only calling about the next shipment.

"No, I'm calling on another matter. The last time I spoke with you about Rossi, you told me you handled the problem."

"Surely there are no worries anymore. Is there a problem?" Moretti asked, concerned.

"Yeah, there is! Some mutha fucker snatched up my lady friend and want a quarter mil to get her back. I spoke with the man on her phone, and I'm sure he was Spanish or Italian, so I just wanted to make sure your man Rossi didn't change his mind," Real spat heatedly as he neared his exit.

"Real, one thing about the families is that we are judged heavily by our loyalty and our word. The old man Rossi would never go against the family's demands. I'm pretty sure Rossi wants to live out the rest of his days. I can give you my word, Real. This end is clear. If you need my help, let me know. I have good men that are very loyal to me," Moretti told Real as he sat on his back balcony looking out over the ocean.

"I appreciate it, but I got everything under control. I'm just trying to find out who's behind this so I'll know who to kill when this shit is over," Real said forcefully as he exited the expressway with B-Low and Jesse tailing him.

"I'm pretty sure you will find your man. Call me if you need me," Moretti said as he entered the call.

After hanging up the phone, Moretti thought about all the kilos he had just dropped to Real. He then looked back on why he hated dealing with Black men. They were too quick to kill without thinking things through. He swore under his breath, hoping Real lived to pay him.

Real turned on the road leading to the golf course. B-Low and Jesse followed close behind. They planned to bypass the course and find a spot up the road to keep a close eye out on Real as he made the transaction.

As Real rounded the corner, all he saw was emergency vehicles and police lights. "Shit! Road block," Real cursed to himself as he reached over and grabbed the bag of money and placed it in the back on the floor before he slowed the truck down.

Getting closer, he saw that it wasn't a road block after all. A car had run off the road and down the embankment. An officer stood in the middle of the street, waving traffic by. As Real passed by the scene with B-Low and Jesse following close behind, they came up on the golf course. To their surprise, there were blue lights and emergency vehicles up there as well. Real had a funny feeling something was wrong. Bypassing the course, he kept straight until he reached the brightly lit Waffle House. He turned into the Waffle House parking and pulled out his cell phone to call

Constance's phone.

A man answered in a heavy Southern drawl. "Hello?"

All Real could hear were sirens and police radios. He knew then that Constance was in the midst of the blue lights. His heart raced as he questioned the man.

"I'm looking for my wife. Who is this? Is she okay?" Real asked firmly.

"Your wife was abducted by two men, but she's fine. One of our units came across them and more than likely saved her life. The poor boy wasn't so lucky himself. Your wife is being taken to Grady Hospital for some minor bruises, but overall, she's fine," the officer explained.

"What? I'm on my way. Thanks!" Real shouted, playing the part. He was more than happy to hear that Constance wasn't hurt. He took a deep breath and smiled.

"What's the move, because shit looking real crazy back there?" B-Low asked.

"I just found out the police got to the kidnappers before we did. They're taking my old lady to the hospital now. She's cool. I'm going to have Cash shoot y'all a lil' extra for your time," Real told them as he placed the truck in reverse.

"Shit! That's all good both ways, and good looking, people," B-Low said as Real turned the truck around and burnt rubber out of the parking lot.

Looking through the glass window at the people being served, B-Low and Jesse decided to grab a bite to eat before they headed back. They had a bad case of the munchies, thanks to the cush.

"I'll take a smothered, covered, chunked sirloin, well done… and a Sprite with no ice," Jesse told the old White waitress that looked at him with disgust as he ordered.

"You, sir?" she asked B-Low with pen and pad in hand.

"Cheeseburger, regular hash browns, and a Coke," B-Low uttered, high on the cush. She wrote down his order and walked off.

"Man, I need a quick come up. You see how that nigga Real rolling? The nigga got a club, moving much weight, all kind of whips…and I can imagine how his house sitting," Jesse said out of the blue.

"Man, I ain't going to lie. I was thinking about the same thang. On the one, bro, I'm fixing to retire the pistol and get me some work. Shit, we'll make way mo' money putting down work!" B-Low said with enthusiasm.

"I'm going to holla at Cash tomorrow and see what he can do for a nigga," Jesse said as the old White lady returned to the table with their drinks.

"Man, fuck talking to Cash. We need to get at that nigga Real," B-Low shot back.

"Naw, bro. It'll be better going through Cash. We'll make him feel like he ain't got no choice because of all the work we done put in for 'im. Then you know Real ain't going to just come out and fuck wit us like that. Today was the first time I ever really heard the nigga talk. Man, straight up, we got to holla at Cash," Jesse insisted.

"Yeah, I feel ya. I'm going to get at him first thang in the morning. Fuck this pistol play. I'm ready to get some real money," B-Low barked as the old White lady sat their plates on the table.

$\mathcal{R}$eal jumped back on the expressway and pushed 120 all the way out to Grady Hospital. On the way, he called Cash.

"Yo, Cash, everything good? Some kind of way the police got involved, but Constance is okay. I'm on my way out to Grady to get her now," Real told Cash in an upbeat tone.

Cash's first thought went to the wire he wore. "That's cool, bro. Did you ever find out who was behind all this shit?" Cash inquired.

"Man, I don't know. After I get Constance, she'll fill me in. I'll make sure I keep you posted," Real said as he neared his exit.

"Yeah, make sure you do that," Cash replied as he pulled up at the stash house. He pulled his cell phone from his pocket. He dialed Trey's number after he unlocked the door and stepped in. Trey was a young dealer from the west side of Atlanta that usually bought three or more blocks every trip.

"Say, young Trey, how many you working with?" Cash asked, feeling real awkward knowing the feds were listening in.

Cash had been contemplating removing the wire long ago and just taking his chances. Throwing the idea around now, he thought back on the papers he signed and remembered the twenty kilos they no longer had. *Hell, they don't have anything, for that matter,* he reasoned. Standing inside the stash house on the phone, he came to the conclusion. *Fuck the feds!* And snatched the wire off. "I'll be out your way about five," Cash told Trey as he hung up the phone and threw the wire in the trash.

A few minutes later, he was loading up the contents of the stash house, planning to just take everything and disappear. Now that he was wireless, he knew the feds would be curious, but he figured he would have enough time in between to pack up and get away.

After packing and loading up all the dope, Cash jumped in the LeBaron and hurried out to his house. There, he transferred all the dope into his brand new Jaguar XJ Supersport and rushed in the house to get what he needed. He packed the Jaguar with his clothes and other property and then double checked everything to make sure he was good to go. Satisfied that everything was in order, he started up the car and backed out of the driveway. Before he could get all the way out of the driveway, though, two unmarked cars pulled up and blocked him in.

"Damn!" Cash screamed, slapping the steering wheel. They were on to him.

It was real obvious that he was about to go on the run. He put the car in park and watched the agents jump out of the unmarked cars with guns in hand.

Agent Blakely led the crowd coming his way. "Get out of the car!" Blakely screamed as he pointed his government-issued weapon at Cash.

"Shit," Cash cursed under his breath as he pushed the door open and got out.

"Turn around and put your hands on your head," Agent Blakely barked as the other agents swarmed Cash and handcuffed him.

"Man, what's this shit all about?" Cash screamed as they led him to the unmarked car.

"Mr. Fields, you know what this is all about! You removed the wire, you emptied the stash house, and then you rushed home and pack up. Come on now, Mr. Fields. You and I both know the deal. We don't just listen in… we watch too!" Agent Blakely said as the agents opened the back door of Blakely's car and shoved Cash inside it.

"Man, I don't know what—"

He was cut off as they slammed the car door.

Agent Blakely opened the front door and got in. "Mr. Fields, don't think for one minute that we didn't think this was coming. That's why we wired you daily. We really thought it would have come sooner. We knew you would think that since we no longer had the twenty kilos that we had nothing to charge you with, and you were half right. With the papers you signed, we could only give you five years, and your case was weak. Seeing what we had, we gambled on you and won. If you would have run off the top, you would be only facing five years and a weak case, but now with all the recorded conversations alone, you don't stand a chance. Wanna know the best part?" Agent Blakely paused and smiled. "The best part is, we just got you again with more dope, and being that you went against our agreement, you will be charged accordingly. All in all, you're fucked. All you had to do was cooperate," Blakely laughed as he turned the key in the ignition.

"Man, I wasn't going nowhere! I swear, man! Why would I go this far and then back out?" Cash pleaded as Agent Blakely put the car in drive and took off on the way to the federal building.

ulling up at Grady, Real found a parking space and jumped out of the truck. He rushed inside to find Constance, completely forgetting he still had on his bulletproof vest. Overlooking the stiff feeling the vest gave him, he continued on until he reached the receptionist's desk.

"Could you please give me the location of Constance Simmons?" Real asked the overweight, heavily made up Black woman behind the desk.

"Who?" she asked, balling her face up.

"Constance Simmons?" Real asked again, this time louder.

"Hold on a minute! Calm down, and I'll check," the woman shot back, rolling her eyes as she entered Constance's name in the computer.

Real stood at the desk, impatiently staring the woman down.

"Second floor, Room 241," she called out as she scratched her itching weave.

Real took off without saying a word. Rather than waiting on an elevator, he snatched open the stairwell door and took the steps by twos up to the second floor. Hurrying down the hall, he found Room 241. A police woman was exiting the room.

"Hi. Is this Constance Simmons' room?" Real asked the short, thick, high yellow cute uniformed officer.

"Yes. And you are?" she asked, looking Real up and down. Like many women, she couldn't help being instantly attracted to the tall, dark, exotic man that towered over her.

"I'm her fiancé. Is it okay to go in?" Real asked, picking up on the officer's flirty gestures.

"Yeah. She all yours," she replied as she cuffed the notepad where she had scribbled Constance's account of the evening's events and walked off.

Real didn't give her a second look as he pushed the door open and entered the room. Constance was coming out of the bathroom as he entered.

"Baby!" Constance screamed as she ran over and jumped into his arms, disregarding the bulky vest he wore.

"Boo, you okay?" Real asked, hugging her tight.

"Baby, I didn't think I would live to see tomorrow. I was so scared," Constance said as her voice cracked and her eyes watered.

"I know, boo. Everything is okay now. I swear it'll never happen again," Real said firmly.

"I love you," Constance cried as she held Real tight.

"Come on. Let's get outta here," Real said as he grabbed her by the hand and led her from the room.

On the way out, they stopped by the nurses' station, signed some papers, and headed out to the truck. As they walked through the hospital, Real questioned Constance about the men that had taken her.

"Baby, it was the Italian men from the club the other night. The officer told me one of the men were killed and the other one is still on the run. They had me in some warehouse close to downtown, by the old Kessler's building."

"You sure it was one of the men from the other night?" Real asked, frowning.

"I'm positive. When I was showing him the house, I knew he looked familiar. I just couldn't place him. Then, the crazy fucker hit me in the back of the head and knocked me out," Constance said heatedly as they reached the truck and got in.

Real went from zero to sixty when Constance told him about the men. He felt Moretti had taken him off guard with his guarantee of taking care of the problem. He thought Moretti had clout within the circle, but now Real thought differently. Pissed off, Real snatched up the phone and angrily dialed Moretti's number.

"Hello?" Moretti answered groggily after being awakened by Real's call.

"You said you took care of the problem! My lady said the men from the club the other night are the ones who grabbed her—Rossi's men! I don't know who you talked to about handling this problem, but evidently they didn't give a fuck about what you were talking about. No ifs, ands, or buts, somebody going to pay for this shit!" Real snapped as Constance listened in.

"Hold on, now, Real. Let's be choice with our words, even in anger. I gave specific instructions to Rossi, and if what you are telling me is true, then he will be dealt with accordingly," Moretti said, not liking Real's tone.

"Oh, it's true! Matter of fucking fact, check around. One of his men were killed in the process!" Real said forcefully as Constance laid her seat back to get more comfortable for the ride home.

"Okay, Real. First thing in the morning, I will check into the matter, my friend," Moretti said, thinking to himself all the time that Real wasn't worth the trouble.

"I would truly appreciate it, but don't think for a fucking second that I'm not looking to make them pay," Real spat as he pushed the Range Rover through the night traffic. "Nobody—and I mean nobody—fucks with my business or my lady."

"I totally understand. I will check into the matter first thing in the morning," Moretti assured him as they ended the call.

Checking his bedside clock, Moretti saw that it was close to midnight. Before he fell back to sleep, he thought of several ways to kill Rossi and cut ties with Real.

Chapter 19

" **B**aby, you okay?" Real asked Constance as he leaned over and rubbed her thigh.

"Yeah, I'm okay. Just listening to you," she said, looking over at Real.

"Baby girl, I don't know what I would have done if you would have been hurt," Real said sincerely as he grabbed her hand.

"Real, I don't want you to get in no trouble or do nothing crazy. I know you, Real, so please don't do anything that may take you from me, please," Constance pleaded as she squeezed his hand.

"I ain't going nowhere, I promise," Real replied as he merged the Range into the right lane and exited the freeway.

Constance was excited to be home. She promised herself after the ordeal that she would never take life for granted. She made plans with Real to pick her car up from the house where she was kidnapped from. Ten minutes after exiting the highway, they were pulling up into their driveway. They got out of the truck and hugged all the way up the door and into the house.

"It feels good to be home!" Constance screamed as she headed up to the bedroom to strip down for a long, warm bubble bath.

"Yeah, especially with you here," Real chimed in as he fol-lowed behind her, admiring her wide hips and big ass.

After taking a bath, Constance climbed into bed and snuggled up to Real. An hour later, they were sleep in each other's arms.

* * * * *

The next morning, Real was awakened by the loud ringing of his cell phone. "Yeah?" he answered sleepily.

"Your sources were correct. Rossi's men were the ones behind the kidnapping. The old man swears he had nothing to do with it, which I beg to differ with. His nephew Saul was the one killed. The families are looking into the matter as we speak. We are all waiting to hear from his other nephew Milo. We think he may have been the other man the police have been asking about. As soon as we narrow it down to specifics, we will act accordingly, but in the mean time, it's business as usual," Moretti said in a firm tone while lighting an expensive cigar.

"Business as usual? Fuck that! My lady was kidnapped and almost killed, and you telling me it's business as usual! I ain't going to sit around for Rossi to strike again! I'm going to track his ass down and kill him where he stands!" Real yelled as he sat up in bed.

"There is no need. We will handle the situation within," said Moretti. "You don't have to—"

Real cut in, "Look here, Moretti. With all due respect, I'm not taking your word on the matter no more. My fiancée was kidnapped because of my trust in your word. I got to go at this shit my way now, no questions about it!" Real snapped.

"Real, I'm warning you. If you go after Rossi against the family's will, war will be waged against you, and ultimately, that would eliminate our business agreement and make us enemies," Moretti threatened, angered by Real's defiance.

"I guess it is war then," Real said forcefully, fed up with all Moretti's family talk.

"Look here. You just pay me what you owe me, and we no longer need to do business!" Moretti shouted as he paced back and forth in his multi-million-dollar beachfront home in Miami.

"How about this? I'll pay you back when I get good and damn ready! You're protecting your family at all costs, and let me tell you, I'm doing the same! Pass the word at your next family picnic. Rossi is as good as a dead, along with whoever else stands in the way!" Real barked before he hung up the phone.

Constance rushed in the room after hearing Real yelling.

"Baby? You alright?" she asked as she stood in the middle of the floor in nothing but her panties and tank top.

"Yeah, shit cool. This mutha fucker think he can tell me what to do! Fuck him! I'm going to show all their bitch asses Real ain't to be fucked with, and I ain't paying him shit!" Real screamed as he threw back the covers and got out of bed.

"What's going on? You talking about Moretti, your connect?" Constance asked, confused.

"Yeah, he wants me to sit back and let mutha fuckers gun at me without straightening my business. He got me fucked up! I'm going to start with Rossi, and then, if anybody else want some, I'll end with them! I'm tired of these foreign mutha fuckers thinking they run shit! Nobody runs me!" Real screamed as he picked up the phone to call Cash. After getting no answer, he stripped down to get into the shower.

Constance took a deep breath before she spoke. "Real, what are you about to get into? Come on now, baby," Constance said softly as she followed him into the bathroom.

"I'm handling my business, that's what I'm doing. I want you to fly out to your cousin's for a while because—"

"Real, I ain't going nowhere. I'm not trying—"

"Look, just get your shit together," Real barked as he stepped into the shower.

Constance knew Real meant business by his tone. She hadn't seen this side of him in a long time, but hearing him brought back memories of the old Real, the uncompromising and treacherous Real—the Real she didn't miss.

Chapter 20

" $\mathcal{T}$his some fuck shit!" Cash screamed. His words echoed off the wall of the same pissy cell that he was detained in before. Agent Blakely had processed him, escorted him to the cell, locked the door, and headed home for the night. Cash lay down and curled up on the hard steel bench.

The next morning, Cash was awakened by Ross as he opened the cell door and screamed his name. "Corey Fields!"

Cash slowly rolled over on the cold bench. "Yeah?" he answered, groggily rubbing his eyes.

"Come on!" Ross said forcefully as he held the door open for Cash.

It was like déjà vu to Cash. They sat in the same conference room, at the same table, in the same old rickety chairs, but this time, the federal prosecutor grabbed a file off the table and looked at it closely as she spoke. "Mr. Fields, you have already signed papers, so that means you owe me five years of your life already. Now, we've got you on noncompliance with our previous agreement, as well as new charges. Let's add this up…the five you owe me and the time you get for the hundred and I think thirty kilos? Well, Mr. Fields, all things considered, what I can tell you is that you will die in prison," the prosecutor said with emphasis on the word 'die' as she looked up from the file and over at Cash.

Cash's heart dropped. "But, man, I was cooperati—"

Cash was cut off before he could get his words out. "Look here, Mr. Fields. I really just want to run you to trial and be through with it, but Agents Ross and Kincaide have convinced me otherwise. As we all know, we could lock you up and throw away the key, but it won't stop Walker's reigning drug empire. That would only delay it. All in all, we can continue this investigation without your help and eventually get Walker, or you can help us get Walker and save your own ass in the process. Believe me, Mr. Fields… we are going to nail Walker's ass to the cross one way or the other. What's it going to be? You in or not? This is your last chance. Are you willing to get up on the stand and save your ass?" the prosecutor asked forcefully as she slammed the file she was looking at down on the conference table.

Cash knew in his heart that if he didn't cooperate—and fully this time—it was over for him. He didn't have to think long before he answered. "A'ight," Cash mumbled, looking down at his shoes.

"Excuse me, sir?" the prosecutor shouted.

"I said okay. I'm in," Cash replied dryly as he lifted his head and stared at her.

"Good. Now you guys go get Mr. Walker. I think we got enough now with Mr. Fields' cooperation to shut his operation down," the prosecutor told Ross and Kincaide as she got up and stormed out of the room.

After the prosecutor left the room, Ross and Kincaid gathered more incriminating evidence from Cash and then escorted him back to his cell, where he would remain until he was moved to a living unit. He would be held in custody until Real was arrested and brought to trial.

* * * * *

While Cash sat in the holding cell waiting to be moved to a living unit, B-Low and Jesse continuously called him on both of his cell phone numbers and didn't get an answer.

"Man, where this nigga at?" B-Low asked as he and Jesse sat in Jesse's one-bedroom apartment out on MLK.

"Man, just leave the nigga a message. He'll hit back sooner or later," Jesse said as he sat on the broken down couch rolling a blunt.

"Needs to be sooner than later! If he don't hit back in the next few minutes, we going down to G-Spot and see if he around."

"Check. That'll work. Just chill," Jesse said in his old-school pimp voice as he lay back on the couch and lit the blunt.

"Man, you bullshitting. I'm ready to make this shit do what it do," B-Low said as he took a seat next to Jesse on the couch and reached for the blunt of cush.

"Puff, puff, pass, nigga!" B-Low shouted as he grabbed the blunt from Jesse.

An hour had rolled by, and Cash still hadn't returned their call.

"Man, shit! It's been almost an hour. Let's ride out to G-Spot. I know that nigga is probably down there, but if he ain't, we just gonna holla at Real," B-Low said as he got up from the couch and dusted the blunt ashes from his Dickies suit.

"Check dat," Jesse slurred, high off the cush.

Both of them grabbed their pistols off of the old scratched-up wooden coffee table and headed out of the door for the club. They rode slowly down the interstate high off the cush. Scarface had them in full gangsta mode as he screamed his latest ode to the streets out of the Chevy's crackling six by nines. The cush had them moving in slow motion, so slow that the thirty-minute ride took them close to an hour.

As they pulled into the parking lot, they didn't see Real's or Cash's cars. Knowing they would show up sooner or later, the two decided to have a couple of drinks and wait around until they arrived. There was always a lot of fine-ass scenery to watch at G-Spot.

Chapter 21

After his shower, Real slipped on a pair of black jeans and a black t-shirt. He grabbed his cell phone off the nightstand and dialed Cash's number. Still, there was no answer.

Before heading downstairs, he looked in on Constance, who was in the guest room packing. "I'm sorry for screaming at you, baby. All this shit got me on the edge. I just want to keep you out of harm's way. It won't be long. Just give me two weeks to get all this shit straight," Real said as he walked over and hugged Constance from behind.

"I understand. I just want you to be careful," Constance cried as she continued to pack her bags.

"I will, I promise. I'll be downstairs. When you finish, just come on down. I'll drop you off at the airport. Baby, just think of this as a spur-of-the-moment vacation. Your cousin will be glad to have you, especially with the way you spoil them with all the shopping and money you pass around."

"I know, but I just want to be here with you," she said as she wiped the tears from her eyes.

"Two weeks, baby, that's all. I'll be downstairs waiting on you. Don't forget to call your cousin and make sure she's at the airport on time to pick you up," Real said as he left the room.

Constance knew it was probably best for her to get away for a while. She packed up the rest of her clothes and called her cousin out in L.A. to let her know she was on her way out.

"I'm ready!" Constance called out as she came downstairs to Real, who was in his office still trying to locate Cash.

"A'ight. I'm coming," he replied as he left Cash another message telling him to meet him down at the club.

Real locked up behind them, loaded Constance's luggage into the back of the Range Rover, and took off for the airport. On the ride to the airport, he called Cash again, but there was still no answer. Real started to worry because Cash usually called back in minutes.

After he pulled up in the airport parking lot, Real unloaded Constance's luggage and slid the luggage handler a fifty-dollar bill.

"Baby, be careful, please," Constance said as she wrapped her arms around Real, holding him as if she never wanted to let him go.

"I will, boo. Just call me as soon as you get there," Real told her as they kissed passionately.

Their long embrace was forcibly ended when airport security motioned for Real to move his truck.

"A'ight, baby. Love you," Real said as he got back behind the wheel.

"Love you, too, baby," Constance said as she slipped her oversized Chanel shades over her eyes and entered the airport to leave for L.A.

Real navigated the truck through the airport traffic as he headed out to his club. En route, he tried calling Cash again. Still, there was no answer. He made up his mind that something was, in fact, wrong. A few minutes later, he was pulling up into the club parking lot.

The club seemed a bit crowded for so early in the day. As Real made his way through the crowd to his office, he heard someone calling his name from behind.

"Real! Real! Say, homie!" B-Low screamed over T.I. being played on the club surround sound speakers.

Real turned around, already paranoid, to see who was calling him. Focusing in, he saw that it was the men that put in work for Cash by way of himself.

"Yeah, what up?" Real asked in a forceful way, letting the men know he really didn't want to talk to them.

"We need to holla at you, bro. We tried getting at Cash, but he ain't hitting back, so we decided to just holla at you," B-Low said as Jesse listened in on their conversation.

"What's the problem?" Real asked, half trusting the two men.

"Oh, there ain't no problem, bro. We just need your help, bro," Jesse said, still feeling the effects of the cush.

"Help with what?" Real asked curiously.

"Man, we trying to change our game up," B-Low said, cutting in.

"Change your game up?" Real asked as he motioned for them to follow him up to the VIP section of the club. Real didn't trust the men enough to invite them back to his office.

"Yeah, man, we putting down the guns and getting into the dope game, but we need some work," B-Low explained as they stood in the middle of the empty VIP section.

Real was skeptical of the men's request. He had known plenty of their kind before, vultures looking for a quick come up at whoever's expense. He knew the men were straight up killers because they had even killed for him in a roundabout kind of way. He looked from one to the other before he spoke. "What kind of work you talking about?" Real asked, trying to see if they were trying to stunt or trying to make some money in the drug game.

"Bro, it don't matter. Probably something small until we can build some clientele," Jesse said firmly

Listening to Jesse's answer, Real saw that the men were really trying to get in the game.

"Well, look, I got to put some things together first because all kind of crazy shit's going on right now, but as soon as I handle this, uh, little problem, I'll hit y'all up and see about getting y'all some work," Real explained.

"Problem? You need some help?" B-Low asked.

Suddenly, an idea came to Real. *These guys may be just the ticket,* he thought. "Hmm. Come to think of it, y'all just may be able to help me after all. Sit down," Real told them as he started explaining the situation with Rossi and Moretti.

"Bro, enough said. We can drive down there and take care of that and be back by the weekend. All you need to do is give us directions to their spot. Look, man, you don't even have to get your hands dirty. We'll handle this one on the strength that you putting us on," Jesse said, excited to be teaming up with Real.

"A'ight. Let me just get with Cash and tie up some loose ends. Give me y'all numbers," Real said as he pulled out a pen and grabbed a napkin from the table.

"When you holla at Cash, tell 'im he could have hit a nigga back," B-Low said as they all stood to leave.

"I'll be getting with y'all before the night out," Real told them as he exited the VIP room and headed to his office.

"Bro, it's on!" Jesse barked excitedly. "Let's take care of them half-breed bitches and come back and get paid!"

They dismissed the girls who were soliciting dances and headed out the door, prepared to do a whole new kind of damage.

Chapter 22

*A*fter giving up on Cash calling back, Real called Max into his office.

"Say, Max, go over these figures and let me know what we need and what we don't. I got to make a quick run," Real told Max as he got out of his office chair and headed out the door.

"I got you, cuz. Ima do better," he assured his cousin as he took a seat behind Real's desk and started punching numbers in the calculator.

As Real exited the club, three expensively dressed Italian men walked by him into the G-Spot. He ignored them and walked out to his truck and headed out to Cash's house to see what was going on.

Real made it to Cash's house in no time. He noticed Cash's car wasn't home, but there were clothes scattered in the driveway. Pulling up in front of the house, Real got out and rushed up to the door. After knocking and getting no answer, he walked around back and looked in. To his surprise, he saw empty drawers pulled out and the closet door wide open with nothing in it. Taking in the scene inside of the house, Real knew Cash was gone. He jumped back in the truck and sped out to the stash house.

On the way there, Real dialed Cash's number over and over again, but there was still no answer. He pulled up in the stash house carport and looked around for any signs of foul play. Seeing that the coast was clear, he hurried up to the door and entered. As he made his way through the house to the back room, he had an uneasy feeling. *Somethin's just not right here,* he thought. When he entered the back room, his worries were confirmed, and his heart dropped.

That nigga took all the mutha fuckin' dope! "Hell naw!" Real screamed as he frantically ran through the house, room by room, looking for the door. "Fuck-ass nigga!" Real yelled as he ran back out to the truck.

Real couldn't believe Cash had run off with the whole shipment. As Real rode back to the club, he made a mental note to kill Cash, right after he killed Rossi. *Nobody—and I mean nobody—steals from me,* he thought, pounding his fist into the dash board.

While Real was on his way back to the club, the three Italians who had walked right past him were feverishly combing the club looking for him. They discreetly concealed their automatic weapons as they made their rounds to locate Real. "Excuse me, miss. Have you seen the owner?" one of the Italians asked Strawberry, the new big-booty White girl from Seattle.

"Oh, yeah, he back in his office," she told them, not knowing Real had left earlier.

As soon as Strawberry told the men where to find Real, they didn't waste any time rushing in the direction of his office. Once they found the office, the Italians didn't hesitate. They entered the office without knocking, guns drawn. Max was still behind the desk tallying the numbers for Real. As soon as they set their sights on the man behind the desk, they unloaded their silencer-equipped weapons. Max was killed mid-sentence as the bullets pierced through his chest and face. Max fell face down on the expensive handmade cherry oak desk, completely lifeless as the purchase orders turned crimson, soaked with his blood.

The three men casually tucked their weapons back into their expensive suits and exited the office, closing the door behind them. When they got out to the parking lot and into their car, they made a call. "Real is no longer with us," the Italian said in a menacing tone as his partner stuck the key in the ignition.

"Good work. I will see you when you get back," Moretti replied, smiling as he pulled one of his most expensive Cuban cigars from his desk and lit it.

Just as the men were pulling out, Real was pulling in. Real noticed the three Italians from earlier in the brand new Maserati Quattroporte with Florida tags, but this time, they were rushing out of the parking lot instead of going into the club. Real didn't think anything of it, as he couldn't blame the guys for wanting to have a drink and a little peek at the finest-ass dancers in town.

Besides that, Real was too distracted with his own thoughts, mad as hell at Cash's betrayal. He rushed back into the club to his office to make some calls. Ducking and dodging all the complaining dancers and shushing Cream and Strawberry with a wave of his hand, he made it to his office. As he pushed the door open, he lost his breath at the sight of his cousin slumped over his desk, bleeding out all over the paperwork and the cherry finish.

"Oh shit!" Real screamed as he closed the door and quietly stepped to the DJ and told him to announce the club had to be evacuated for unforeseen circumstances.

"What up, boss?" the DJ asked as he packed up his CDs.

"Ain't nothing. I'll holla at you later," Real said, still in a slight daze from seeing his cousin Max's head split open on his desk.

After everybody left, Real dialed 911; the police arrived in a matter of minutes.

An old Black detective scolded Real for closing the club before they arrived, considering that they could have interviewed potential witnesses. The coroner removed Max's body as Real looked on with pure hatred seething inside him for the men that carried the hit out. After the detective questioned Real and gathered evidence, they told him they would be in touch, but Real didn't bother to give them any information because he knew who was behind this, and he wanted them himself.

After seeing the police off, Real went back into his blood-drenched office, emptied the safe, and locked the club doors as he exited. "Mutha fuckers don't know who they fuckin' with! You want a war, fuckers? Well, it's on!" Real declared calmly as he exited the club.

Chapter 23

$\mathcal{C}$ash sat uncomfortably on the holding cell bench thinking back on the good old days when he and Real were living the life. He smiled as he thought back on the women, the clubbing, the money, and the sex-filled nights before Real met Constance. Cash regretted his decision to help the feds bring Real down, but he knew it was his life or Real's. While Cash sat on the bench entertaining thought after thought, his cell door opened.

"Corey Fields, put these on. You're being moved into a protective custody unit per the federal prosecutor," a chubby Black guard announced as he threw Cash some old prison garb in a gaudy orange.

After changing out of his street clothes, Cash was moved to PC—a one-man cell where he would remain until Real was brought in and taken to trial.

* * * * *

While Cash was adjusting to his new home, B-Low and Jesse were sitting around impatiently waiting on Real to call.

Just as B-Low and Jesse started thinking twice about Real's intentions, the phone rang.

"Say, I need y'all to meet me out at my spot ASAP," Real spat, going against his rules of never letting anybody come to his crib. He knew if he was going to deal with Jesse and B-Low, he would have to start trusting them fully.

He gave directions as he pushed the Range Rover to the limit while thinking of his next move. Twenty minutes later, he was pulling up into his driveway and entering his empty house. He walked briskly to his home office and took a seat in his oversized office chair to contemplate his plans.

As Real was sitting behind his desk running his plans through his head over and over again, B-Low and Jesse pulled up. "Man, this is boss as fuck!" Jesse said, looking up at Real's multi-million-dollar home.

"Bro, in due time, we going to be living up in one of these mutha fuckers—just like this one! I told you this nigga was living like a king," B-Low declared as he pulled the Chevy to a halt and killed the engine.

B-Low and Jesse looked on in amazement as they walked up to the door and knocked. A few seconds later, Real was at the door to let them in.

"What it do?" Jesse asked as they entered the house.

"Shit 'bout to get Real crazy around this bitch. I'm going to give all these bitches a taste of the old me," Real said as they walked through the house and down to his office.

B-Low and Jesse were in awe of the expensive furnishings and state-of-the-art electronics that filled the house.

"Bro, we got you. Just give us the rundown, and shit will be taken care of," B-low promised Real as they entered his plush office.

"Take a seat," Real told them as he walked around his desk and sat in his office chair.

"Bro, you ever catch up with Cash?" Jesse asked as he took a seat on the soft black leather couch positioned on the office wall.

"That's part of the problem. That nigga done ran off with my work. He got to be handled too!" Real said firmly.

Hearing Real talking about taking Cash out caught them totally off guard. They were closer to Cash than they were to Real, but when it came down to the money and being down with Real, Cash was a dead man.

"He ran off? Damn, bro. Slimey as fuck! Bro, we will handle all this shit," Jesse said forcefully.

"Listen…this the move…" Real first told them about the men coming in the club and killing Max, and then he ran down the plan. "We—and yeah, I said 'we'—ain't passing up the chance to look in these hoes' faces when I stop them from breathing. We going out to Miami Beach and handle Rossi, and then we going out to Star Island and pay Moretti a visit. I got a friend down that way that's going to give me their locations when we get there. I'm going to send both families a message since I don't know which one is responsible for my cousin's death," Real said as he slid his desk drawer open and pulled out his chrome Desert Eagle.

"Bro, you really don't have to get your hands dirty. We can hit down there and be back in no time," Jesse told Real.

"Man, like I said, I'm going to look in these hoes' faces when they take their last breaths. I'm in no matter what! Nobody—and I mean no fucking body—snatches my lady, steals my shit, and aims their guns at my damn family!" Real said firmly as he ejected the clip and started sliding bullets in it with his signature handkerchief.

"A'ight, bro. When we taking off?" Jesse asked.

"Tomorrow morning. Y'all meet me at the Burger King on Old National. I'll have us a rental car. Y'all got heat?" Real asked them with a raised eyebrow as he cocked back the Desert Eagle.

"Heat? What that rap nigga said? We pack mo heat than the oven door," B-Low declared as he pulled up his shirt, revealing twin nines.

"My bad," Real grinned. "Y'all just meet me at Burger King in the morning at eight so we can reach Miami by six."

"That's a go," B-Low said as he and Jesse stood to leave.

Walking back through the house, B-Low vowed quietly to himself that he would one day own a house like Real's.

* * * * *

After seeing them out the door, Real took a shower and got in the bed. Just as he was dozing off, his phone rang. "Hello?" he answered sleepily.

"Hey, baby! I'm here," Constance said.

"Hey, baby girl! So you finally made, huh?" Real said joyfully, glad to hear his baby's voice.

"Yeah, I'm here. Cuz says 'hey'. Baby, you sound like you were sleep."

"Yeah, it's been a long day. Somebody killed Max in the club in my office," Real told her calmly, as if it were an everyday occurrence.

"Quit playing, Real!" Constance yelled.

"Seriously, he's dead. Some Italian fuckers did it," Real told her as he stared up at the ceiling fan.

"Oh no! Real, you got to get away from all that! Please, baby! Why would they kill Max?" Before the words left her mouth, she thought about what Real said—that they had killed Max *in his office.* She was more than sure that the men took Max to be Real.

Real had already realized the same thing. "They had to think Max was me, being that he sat behind my desk in my office," Real explained as the image of Max lying dead popped up in his head.

"Baby, please be careful," Constance pleaded.

"I will, boo. I'll call you tomorrow. Love you," said Real.

"Love you too," Constance replied as the line went dead.

In no time, Real had drifted off into a deep sleep, dreaming of sweet vengeance.

Chapter 24

The next morning, Real met up with B-Low and Jesse at the Burger King on Old National, just as planned. Not wasting any time, they got situated for the long ride to Miami. Real started off the long stretch behind the wheel as they rotated driving duties every couple of hours.

Ten hours later, they were exiting off at Miami Beach and pulling into a Quick Mart parking lot. Real pulled out his cell phone and called his Miami connect, Sergio.

"My man Real! How's it going?" asked one of the biggest money launderers in the South.

Real dealt with Sergio on a regular basis, and it was good to hear his voice again. "Just exited off at Miami Beach. What you got for me?" Real asked as he grabbed a pen and piece paper from the car console.

"Well, Moretti was quite easy to locate, as a matter of fact. You're already in his neighborhood. He's got a house out on the beach, but you can surely find him at his lil' Italian eatery out by Royal Palm Ave. The name of the place is Papino's, and he makes it his business to go over his books every night while having dinner there. He's usually with his nephew Angelo and his brother Carlo," Sergio said as he flipped the page on his notepad.

"Okay, got it," Real uttered as he took notes.

"The other man—this Rossi—was a little harder to locate, but I found him. He's got a mansion out in Coral Gables, which he hardly ever leaves. You got a pen, right? His address is 2736 Coral Way. He stays there with his nephews Alberto, Saul, and Milo. Word is, the police killed one of them, and the other's gone AWOL. They frequented Atlanta a lot on business. But anyway, Rossi's place is used for most of the family meetings. I checked to see where he could be found on a regular basis but came up empty handed. The man is a fucking hermit. He rarely leaves the house. That's the best that I could do for you, old friend," Sergio said, closing the notepad as he walked through his multi-million-dollar home on LaGorce Island.

"Naw, that's more than enough info. I appreciate it, Sergio. I'll get back with you later," Real said as ripped the notes from his pad.

"Anytime. Just remember…you didn't hear it from me," Sergio declared. He knew it would be an automatic death sentence if anyone found out he divulged this information.

"I got you. I'll get at you," Real assured him as he ended the call.

"A'ight, y'all," Real said to B-Low and Jesse, who had been loading their weapons while he spoke with Sergio, "this is what we got. Moretti can be found at his restaurant right around the corner from here, and this old Rossi fucker can be found out in Coral Gables. It ain't that far, but we got to get in his house to touch him," Real explained as he looked back down at his notes.

"No problem. Who we takin' out first?" B-Low asked as he loaded his two nines.

"I think we should holla at Rossi first and then come around and see Moretti. We got to catch Moretti in his restaurant, which is a public spot, and that ain't good. We will see him last because we don't know what kind of heat it's going to bring," Real explained.

"I feel that," Jesse added as he stuffed shell cartridges into his pistol grip pump.

"Let's do this," Real said as he put the black rented Lincoln Town Car in drive and cruised out of the parking lot.

The factory navigational system led them right to Rossi's front door. B-Low and Jesse instantly realized that Real's mansion was a shack compared to Rossi's palace. Real pulled the Lincoln next to the curb just outside of the residence.

"How in the hell we going to find him in there?" Jesse asked as he pulled out three ski masks. "This house is big as hell."

"We going to grab the first mutha fucker we see and make 'im take us to the asshole!" Real said forcefully.

"Yeah. When we move, we got to move fast, because we don't know who off in there.. and most importantly—rule number one..." B-Low said.

"...leave no witnesses," Jesse added, cutting him off.

"I always follow the rules," Real agreed, smiling deviously as he reached back and plucked the black ski mask out of Jesse's hand.

Just as they were about to exit the car, a big black and grey Maybach cruised by them and turned into Rossi's driveway. After the car stopped, all the occupants piled out. Real and his boys knew the old man had to be Rossi by the way the housekeepers and the driver hastily came to his aide to accommodate him. The muscle-bound man that got out behind him was his nephew, Alberto, who doubled as a body guard from time to time. Real, B-Low, and Jesse knew this was their best shot, being that the house was in a secluded area with no one around. Trying to get into the house was going to be difficult, but catching him now was going to be real easy.

"Now or never!" Real called out as he pulled the ski mask over his head and grabbed his Desert Eagle off the seat.

"Shit! Let's do the damn thang!" B-Low screamed as he adjusted the ski mask around his eyes.

"Let's ride!" Jesse chimed in as he pulled his ski mask down.

Geeked for the kill, all three men jumped out of the Lincoln and rushed the Italians, who were standing in the driveway next to the Maybach laughing and talking. When the Italians saw the three men in ski masks rounding the corner with guns raised, their eyes grew big as golf balls.

"Yeah, bitches!" B-Low screamed as he ran up on Rossi's nephew Alberto and shot him at point blank range in the face. Alberto never had a chance to pull his forty-five automatic secured in his wrap around holster.

Jess caught the driver with the pistol grip pump in the back as he started to run. It blew him clean off his feet and into the grass. The two Italian female housekeepers screamed at the top of their lungs until Real silenced each of them with a bullet to the chest.

Old man Rossi tried his best to make it to the house; he hopped as far as he could before Real ran him down. Blocking the old man's path to the house, Real hit him hard in the head with the Desert Eagle knocking him to the ground as B-Low and Jesse looked on. "You sent men to kill me! You fuckin' threaten me! You kidnap my girl!" Real screamed as he stood over a cowering Rossi.

"No! No! No! I don't know what you are speaking of!" Rossi screamed, holding his wrinkled hands up in front of his face as he lay face up in the grass.

"Fuck, bitch, THIS is what I'm speaking of!" Real screamed as he knocked the old man's hands out of the way and placed the barrel of the Desert Eagle in the middle of his forehead.

"No! I swear! Please! I don't know who—" Rossi begged.

"Fuck you, bitch!" Real shouted as he pulled the trigger, literally blowing off Rossi's face. Rossi's blood splattered into Real's face, drenching his ski mask.

B-Low and Jesse were both cold-hearted killers, but the sight of Rossi's face being blown away even disturbed them. They knew right then that the laid back, quiet Real was a stone-cold killer also.

They followed rule number one. Leaving no witnesses, they all rushed back out to the Lincoln and sped off to the next stop on their to-do list of vengeances.

Chapter 25

*W*heeling the Lincoln away from Coral Gables, they headed out toward Royal Palm Avenue, where they knew Moretti would be having dinner and going over his books. Pushing the Lincoln in and out of traffic, they reached the eatery in no time.

"The place looks empty," Jesse noticed as they circled the restaurant parking lot.

"Probably a lil' family spot. I'm going to peep in and see if I see him," Real said, pulling the car to the far end of the lot before getting out and adjusting his clothes, trying his best to disguise the old man's blood on his shirt. He adjusted his Desert Eagle in his waist as he walked briskly across the lot.

B-Low and Jesse sat in the car loading their weapons as they waited on a signal from Real to move in. While watching Real, they paid no attention to one of Moretti's men creeping up from behind, pistol in hand. Sergio failed to tell them that Moretti kept security at the eatery and an unknown car in the lot alone would be suspicious.

Real lightly jogged up to the eatery and positioned himself on the side of the building. Looking around to make sure the coast was clear, he rounded the corner and peeped into the window. He saw Moretti sitting at a far corner table with two other men, talking. Knowing B-Low and Jesse were watching, he waved them over without taking his eyes off the men and Moretti. As Real evaluated the scene, he knew he could get a drop on the men at the table, but the old cook in the back would be a problem. Real knew that even old Italian cooks could be armed and dangerous. He decided to take the cook out first. Real watched the men intently while he waited for B-Low and Jesse to get across the lot.

Just as B-Low and Jesse got out of the car, the man with the gun eased up on them, nice and slow. "Don't move! Both of you drop the guns!" he screamed from behind them as he used his free hand to fish his cell phone from his pocket.

Jesse and B-Low stopped in their tracks when they heard the man behind them. "What's the problem, sir?" B-Low asked as he dropped his gun to the ground.

"Yeah, what's going on?" Jesse added as he let the pistol grip hit the pavement.

"Don't fuckin' move!" the man yelled forcefully again.

"Look here, man…we just trying to get a lil' something to eat," Jesse lied, knowing deep down the man wasn't buying it, especially considering they were brandishing guns.

"Put Mr. Moretti on," the man barked into the cell phone while holding the gun steady at B-Low and Jesse.

Real looked over to see what was taking B-Low and Jesse so long, and that's when he saw the man with the gun on them. "Shit!" Real said under his breath as he ducked back around the building.

A few minutes later, Moretti and the two men from inside busted out of the eatery door, looking for the men his security called him about. Real knew if he didn't act quickly, B-Low and Jesse would be killed by Moretti and his men. Just as Moretti and the two men stepped off the curb, Real let loose on them, all the while hoping Jesse and B-Low had managed to get a drop on the men with the gun on them.

Pop! Pop! Pop!

Real hit the first man in the leg, causing him to go down, just as the second man took off running. Moretti couldn't move quickly enough. Real hit him in the stomach, doubling him over. Not wasting any time, Real ran up on Moretti and looked him dead in the face as he tried to speak.

"You were…killed…" Moretti uttered as he looked up, clutching his stomach and curling into a grotesque contortion somewhat like a fetal position.

"Naw, bitch, YOU were killed!" Real spat as he put a single shot to Moretti's temple and one to the chest of the other wounded man.

Caught up in the moment, Real didn't realize Jesse had been shot. B-Low stood over the dead gunman with his nine in his hand.

Just as Real started into their direction, a speeding car rounded the corner. Real took off, running full speed to the Lincoln as the men fired shots at him.

B-Low, seeing the men coming frantically, tried to pick Jesse up to get him in the car.

"Come on, man! Let's get the fuck outta here!" Real shouted as he reached the car and jumped behind the wheel.

"Bro, you going to make it! Get up, bro!" B-low screamed at Jesse, who was unconscious and bleeding profusely.

The men in the car were closing in fast, shooting round after round in their direction. B-Low knew if he didn't make a move soon, he would be killed. He had no choice but to leave Jesse behind.

"Drive! Drive!" B-low screamed as he jumped in the car. He took one last glance back at his partner, lying wounded in the parking lot.

Real hit the gas on the Lincoln and sped out of the lot with the angry Italians still trailing behind them. The men in the car gave chase until they heard sirens coming in their direction. Realizing they couldn't catch Real, the italians turned around, rushed back to the lot, and loaded a wounded Jesse in their car before they sped off.

Chapter 26

*W*ord had spread fast in the Italian community that the heads of two of the most powerful families had been gunned down. No one knew who was responsible for the murders, but word around Miami's underground was that the Moretti family had picked up one of the men involved and was nursing him to health just to question him to find out who sent the hit.

Moretti's nephew Angelo instructed his men to keep a close eye on Jesse while he recuperated. The day after the murder of Moretti, Angelo was appointed to lead the family.

Milo, who was hiding out in Atlanta, heard about his uncle's death through one of his close friends in Miami. Milo's dreams had finally come true, and he knew he would now lead his family back into power. He knew everyone was wondering where he was, so he came up with an out-of-the-country story to satisfy everyone's curiosity. After the dust had settled a bit, he planned to settle into his rightful position as head of the family. He wasted no time making his way back to Miami.

* * * * *

It had been two days since the murders, and Real still hadn't heard from B-Low since dropping him off at his car at Burger

King. Real knew how distraught B-Low was over leaving Jesse in the parking lot, and they were both sure Jesse had been killed.

Real knew the families would never suspect him, being that he was confirmed dead, and since Jesse was certainly dead by now and couldn't talk, he wasn't worrying about retaliation. Now, all he wanted to do was track Cash down and punish him for his disloyalty. He picked up the phone on his desk and called a couple of his best resources, but after hanging up the phone, he still didn't have a clue where Cash was.

Getting his head back in the game, Real contemplated on a new connect, being that Moretti was dead. After thinking for a minute, he picked up the phone and called Pam, a former connect who was from the north side of Atlanta. Pams's prices weren't as low as Moretti's, but she could drop it by the loads.

Pam and Real went way back, even before Real and Constance. At one time, they were an item, but they never let their personal relationship interfere with their business. Pam called it quits after catching Real cheating for the third time. After the breakup, Real and Pam agreed to remain friends.

Pam was known around the city as a boss bitch that would kill anybody who disrespected her in any way. Her rough interior didn't come close to matching her outer beauty. Pam was the spitting image of Lauren London, complete with a big, round ass. She was one of the finest, classiest women in the city and kept her chrome 380 tucked in her waist at all times.

"Pam," Real said into his office phone.

"Real," Pam replied, happy to hear his voice.

Real didn't know Pam had taken a couple of bad licks these last few days. The lick that ultimately took her out of the game had come just the day before, when she called her Miami connect to confirm the 200-kilo shipment that she had paid for in advance. After calling time and time again, finally someone answered her connect's phone and told her that her connect had been killed outside of his house. The person who answered the phone then hung up, and no one had answered the phone since.

"What's up? What you been up too?" Real asked, thinking about old times with Pam.

"I've been doing. Jus' still trying to live in this man's world," Pam replied jokingly.

"I'm trying to buy a house. You got one for sale?" Real asked in code, knowing Pam would catch on.

"Yeah. What's your price range, and how many rooms you looking for?" Pam asked, knowing full well that she couldn't produce.

"I'm looking in the range of $1.5 mill, around thirteen rooms," Real said, doing the math in his head.

"Okay. I can find one for that, no problem. Give me a few minutes, and I'll hit you back." Pam hung up the phone, now desperate for a come up. She had agreed to Real's price but had other plans for his money. She knew Real would pay up front, so she planned to take the $1.5 mill and flip it with her Florida connect, and then double back and get Real his package.

Real walked over to his safe and pulled two stacks of money out at a time until he had the $1.5 million. As he counted the money, he got madder and madder at Cash. He thought back on the days when Cash wasn't buying but two and a baby, driving around in an old Monte Carlo. Now, after Real's assistance, he was a major player in the game. Shaking his head in disgust, he continued to count out the $1.5 million, taking no notice of the feds and DEA agents surrounding his house like ants on a picnic.

As Real counted, he picked up his desk phone and called Constance. "Hey, boo," Real said with enthusiasm, happy to hear her voice.

"Hey, baby! Is everything okay?'" Constance asked, also happy to have Real on the phone, alive and well.

"Yeah, boo, everything cool," Real assured her.

"Cool enough for me to come home now?" Constance asked in a hopeful tone.

"Yeah. It's cool enough for my baby to come back home," Real told her as he continued to count the money. "God, I've missed you."

Before Constance could reply, FBI and DEA agents stormed the house. Real dropped the phone when he heard the loud *crash* and glass shattering. Knowing that he didn't have enough time to get out of his office, he had no choice but to barricade the thick wooden door.

"FBI! Come out now with your hands up!" the burly agent screamed as they combed the house looking for Real.

Real was half relieved it was only the FBI and not a gang of Italian killers. Real knew he couldn't get away, so he packed the money back into his safe and grabbed the phone, where Constance was still holding on, listening in on all the commotion and probably scared out of her mind. "Baby, the police in the house. Come on home and get with our lawyer and—"

CRASH! The door flew open.

When Real looked up, all he saw was an arsenal of government-issued guns pointed squarely at every inch of his head and body. He dropped the phone and put his hands up.

Constance was on the next flight home.

Chapter 27

" Everyone, can I please have your attention!" Milo screamed across the grand room in what was once Rossi's house but was now his.

All the heads of the families were brought together to discuss the murders of two of their most powerful leaders. Milo had called the meeting after arriving back in Miami and being placed at the head of the family. Discussing the murders wasn't Milo's main objective though. His main intention for the meeting was to make sure everyone knew he was in charge of the Rossi family and also to show the other families that the Rossi family was about to regain the powerful position it once held.

"We understand Angelo has one of the men who were involved in the murders. Angelo, is the man talking yet?" Milo asked Angelo, who sat at the far end of the table.

Angelo was also recently appointed to the head of the Moretti family. Angelo was determined to avenge his uncle's death at all costs. The other families had the utmost respect for Angelo—way more than they would ever have for Milo, whom they all knew was a self-serving loose cannon. "Yes," Angelo answered, "we do have one of the men involved. He's still sedated, but as soon as he comes to, we will most definitely get him to reveal his sources,"

Angelo said with confidence as he took a sip of the ridiculously expensive ancient red wine that was placed in front of every man at the table.

"Good, good. So, by the end of the week, we should have some answers then?" Milo questioned.

"Don't know. Like I said before, he is sedated. When he comes to, we will question him. I will most definitely keep all the families informed," Angelo said firmly.

"Good. So, do we have everyone's cooperation in going after the men behind the murders?" Milo asked as he looked at each man at the table.

"You got my help," said Carlo, head of the Romano family.

"Mine too," Uberto, head of the Bianchi family added.

Before long, all the men in the room had agreed to come together and destroy the men behind Mr. Moretti's and Mr. Rossi's deaths.

After going over a couple more issues concerning the cartel, they all called it a night. After seeing everyone out, Milo went up to his room, which was once Rossi's old room. He sat in the oversized expensive leather chair, lit an expensive cigar, and smiled, basking in the pride that came with knowing he had gotten his way. He was finally in power.

As Angelo drove home, he thought about how Milo was going to bring tension within the cartel with his unscrupulous ways. Milo voted against him heading the Rossi family, but all the other heads knew he was the only one in the family who was well versed in the dealings with the cartel. Angelo knew that, in due time, Milo would destroy the whole Rossi family legacy with his so-called 'power tactics'. Angelo shook his head at the thought as he pulled up into his driveway thirty minutes later.

Before he could get out of the car, one of his men ran out the door to meet him. "Angelo, the man is conscience, but he claims he doesn't remember anything."

"Oh yeah? Well, let's see if we can help jar his memory a little," Angelo said as they entered the house and headed straight for the wine cellar, where they had Jesse tied up to a makeshift bed.

Jesse looked around in shock at his surroundings. After a minute, he remembered how he was lying out in the parking lot, bleeding from the gunshot wound and then all of a sudden blacked out. He wondered where he was and how he got there. He snatched at the rope and saw it was no use. The Italian men that sat flanking the bed with automatic weapons just stared at him.

"Hey there, friend. Do you know who I am?" Angelo asked Jesse, who lay in the uncomfortable bed, confused and in pain.

"No. Who the hell are you, and how did I get here?" Jesse asked, now realizing that the men in the room had to be linked to the Italians they had killed.

"We can do this the easy way or the hard way, my friend. The easy way is you can tell who sent you, and the hard way is I can *make* you tell me who sent you," Angelo spat.

"Man, I don't know nothing. I came—"

Angelo's hand across his face caught him totally off guard. "Look here, you Black piece of shit! Who sent you?" Angelo demanded as he dug into his inside jacket pocket and pulled out a menacing-looking switchblade.

"Look, man, I was brought into this by a friend. I don't know who he works for," Jesse lied, protecting Real who was surely going to put him on when he got out of there.

"Okay," Angelo said deviously. Reaching back into his pocket, he pulled out a cigarette lighter. He struck it and held the flame to the tip of the blade until it turned red hot. Then Angelo ran the tip of the blade down the side of Jesse's face.

"Ahhh!" Jesse screamed out in pain.

"Who the fuck sent you?" Angelo screamed as he heated the blade again. This time, he pressed it into Jesse's mouth, burning his lips as Jesse tried to press his lips together tight so the knife couldn't enter.

"Ahhh! Umm! Umm!" Jesse screamed as he held his mouth

closed.

Angelo heated the blade once again. This time, Angelo pressed the blade into Jesse's eye.

"Ahhh! Okay! Okay!" Jesse screamed.

"Who the fuck sent you?" Angelo calmly asked again as reheated the blade.

"Real!" Jesse exclaimed, dropping his head back on the stained raggedy pillow.

"You liar. Real's dead," Angelo said as he positioned the blade over Jesse's other eye.

"No! No, man! I swear! Your guys fucked up, man. The man y'all killed in the club was his cousin Max, who managed the club for him!" Jesse explained, moving his head away from the blade of the knife.

Angelo looked around at his men—the same men that had supposedly killed Real.

"We killed him, Angelo. Right in his office, we swear," one of the men said in a panicked tone.

"Did you know for a fact that it was him?" Angelo asked firmly.

Both men looked at each other, and then the first man answered. "No, but one of those strippers said he was in—"

Angelo knew then that Jesse was telling the truth. Satisfied with Jesse's confession, Angelo walked over to the man holding a forty-five automatic. "Give me your gun." Angelo demanded. Gun in hand, he walked back over to Jesse in the bed. "You fuckin' piece of shit!" Angelo screamed as he put a single bullet in the middle of Jesse's forehead.

After killing Jesse, Angelo went upstairs and reached out to every member of the family. He filled them in on Jesse's revelations, and, in turn, all the families summoned some of their best men to head up to Atlanta to eliminate Real and anybody close to him.

Chapter 28

The next day, Constance contacted Real's lawyer, Todd Maddox, one of Atlanta's best criminal attorneys. An hour later, they were rushing down to the federal building together. Pulling up into the federal parking lot in Todd's Lexus 460, Constance and Todd parked and rushed through the double glass doors.

Todd flashed his credentials, and a few minutes later, he was in an expensively furnished office, talking to the U.S. attorney about Real's arrest. Constance waited for him out front. Todd found out that Real was being held on a number of charges, and the State's attorney was most definitely going to seek a RICO indictment. Todd also knew they would file an injunction to seize all property and bank accounts pending the trial outcome.

After hearing Real's charges, Todd exited the office and filled Constance in on the way downstairs to see Real. They approached the old White lady guard that sat behind the desk and gave her Real's name. A few minutes later, the attorney visit was confirmed.

"Ma'am, you can't go back. Only the attorney is allowed in the visiting area," the old lady told Constance as she pressed the button to open the door.

"What? But I really need to see him," Constance pleaded.

"Sorry, ma'am. Only legal counsel is allowed at this hour.

You will have to come back during his family visiting hours on weekends," the old lady said sternly.

"It's okay," Todd assured Constance. "I'll go back and see what's going on. You just hang out here for a minute. I'll let him know you are out here."

Constance paced the floor in the federal building lobby, really hating the old lady guard for not letting her back to see Real.

Todd was led by a short stocky male guard down the hall to a small enclosed room with two chairs and a desk.

After securing Todd in the room, the guard went and got Real from the holding cell, where he had been lying on the cold steel bench with his shirt balled up under his head for a pillow. "Richard Walker, your attorney is here!" the man yelled.

"A'ight," Real snapped back as he sat up, unballed his shirt, and put it on.

When Real was brought in, Agents Kincaide and Ross tried the good cop/bad cop routine just to see if they could get any information out of him. After giving up, they had locked him back in the holding cell. Little did Real know that Cash was right above him in a PC cell waiting to testify against him.

"Put your hands on the wall," the guard instructed Real as he patted him down and then handcuffed him before walking out of the cell. The guard led Real down the hallway to the small enclosed room where Todd patiently waited.

"Hi there, Richard. How's it going?" Todd asked as Real and the guard entered the room

The guard uncuffed Real and then exited the room, carefully closing and locking the door while Real and Todd discussed the charges brought against Real.

"What's going on here, Todd? Where is Constance?" Real asked worriedly.

"Constance is out front. They wouldn't let her back. Sit down and let me fill you in on what I know."

Real told Todd as they took a seat face to face in the hard

wooden chairs that were divided by an old wooden office desk. "Man, I can't believe this shit," Real said, rubbing his head.

"Look, this is what's going on. First, they are more than likely going to get you indicted on the RICO Act and have all of your assets and accounts seized until all of this is over. Hopefully, it's not too late for Constance to pull your money before the injunction is signed off on. Second... well, the truth is, I don't really know what all they got on you right now, but I'll find out in due time so we can prepare. Third—and most importantly—we're going to do everything we can to get you up out of here," Todd said forcefully, looking at Real over the rims of his gold-framed glasses.

"Man, they can't have too much. I'm very discreet in everything I do," Real assured Todd.

"Real, being totally honest with you, the way the U.S. attorney is talking, they got more than enough—especially coming after you with the RICO Act. You are probably not too familiar with the RICO, so let me explain. A RICO-related charge is considered easy to prove in court because it focuses on patterns of behavior as opposed to criminal acts," Todd explained as Real slumped down into his chair.

"Todd, look, I need you to pull all of the strings you can to get me out of here. I don't care what the cost. I will pay you one way or the other," Real said as he stood up and started pacing back and forth in the small room.

"I'm going to dig deep and find out everything they've got. Just give me a couple of days. In the mean time, we are going to try to get you a bond."

"A'ight. Man, I need you to beat this shit for me," Real said adamantly.

"I'm going to do everything in my power. You have my word," Todd assured Real as he stood at the door, signaling for the guard to open it.

"I appreciate it, man... and tell my baby I love her," Real said as Todd walked out the door with a reassuring nod.

The guard locked Real in the room while he escorted Todd back to the front. A few minutes later, the guard was back to get Real. After the same pat-down routine, Real was escorted back to the holding cell.

While Real was being escorted back to the holding cell, Cash was upstairs getting the news from a guard that Real had been arrested and brought in.

Chapter 29

*F*our days later, a black Chevy Tahoe with four men in it pulled into the G-Spot parking lot. Seeing that the club was closed, the driver picked up his cell phone and placed a call. "The place is closed," he said. "You got any more info on him?" he asked Milo.

"Not at this time. Let me make a few calls and call you right back," Milo said as he looked through his Rolodex for the number of his Italian connect in the Atlanta police department.

Milo was surprised at the news he got from his APD connect, who told him Real was locked up and being held at the Atlanta federal holding facility, awaiting trial on numerous charges. Milo called the men off and made a call to Angelo .

"I don't care where the fuck he is, he is still going to pay," Angelo told Milo forcefully.

"I agree. His trial is in a couple of weeks. I will follow it closely," Milo said, pondering how he might get at Real in prison.

"Okay, and if he's found guilty, I have connections on the inside that will gladly take care of him for a small fee," Angelo said menacingly. "Hell, some of those guys will whack somebody for a fucking pack of cigarettes."

"Good. I will let you know the outcome," Milo said, ending the call.

In the heart of Atlanta, Constance was getting ready to go

visit Real. She was no longer staying in the mansion. She had purchased a modest two-bedroom condo early in the week when the feds filed the injunction on all of Real's property and assets. The only things she was left with were her Bentley and her bank account, which was well over a million bucks. She was glad Real had taken her advice and invested. She cashed out all of the stock listed in her name and added the $4.5 million to her bank account also.

Constance made her way down to the federal building to see Real. Pulling into the parking lot, she found the first empty space and parked. As she eagerly headed up to the door to see her lover, she almost broke a heel rushing to get in. She showed her identification to the overweight Black woman working the desk. After looking Constance's name up on the computer to make sure she was on Real's visitation list, the woman pushed the button that opened the glass double doors that led to the visitation area.

A guard escorted Constance to the visiting room, where she was seated behind a glass wall as she waited patiently for Real to come out. A few minutes later, Real was brought in. He was dressed in a prison jumpsuit and seated on the other side of the glass.

"Hey, baby!" Constance yelled as her eyes began to water.

"Hey, boo," Real smiled, looking through the glass at his beautiful Constance.

"How are you doing, baby? I want you home! Why haven't you called?" Constance asked.

"They won't let me use the phone yet. What is going on? What is Todd doing?" Real asked, concerned.

"Baby, they took everything. I had to get a condo downtown. They got the house, all the cars—well, except for my Bentley— and they froze your accounts. They got everything, baby! Todd said he is working on a bond. I... I just don't know what to do," Constance said as she broke down and started crying.

"I figured it would happen sooner or later. Todd had warned

me. Don't worry about it, baby. Everything is going to be alright," Real said, assuring Constance with a strong voice, even though he wasn't so sure himself.

"I hope so," Constance cried.

"Everything else okay?"

"Yes. Oh…a guy named B-Low came by the house when the movers were packing everything. I figured it was okay to tell him about the situation, being that he knew where we stayed, so I knew you trusted him. He gave me a number to give to you," Constance said as she wiped the tears from her eyes.

"A'ight. Just hold onto that number. When they move me upstairs, I'll be able to use the phone, and I'll call him then," Real said.

They talked a little more about the case, and time flew by. Before they knew it, the guard was knocking on Real's door to let him know the short visitation was over with.

"Dang," Constance sighed, hating to leave.

"You hold your head up, baby. We got this! I promise you I'll be home soon," Real said with confidence as Constance stood to leave.

"I hope so. I love you," Constance said sadly as she got up to leave.

"Love you too," Real replied and smiled, though he was crying on the inside.

Chapter 30

One Month Later…

*A*fter being denied bond, Real was moved upstairs to a regular housing unit. He had reached out to B-Low but kept his conversation short just in case the feds were listening in. He gave B-Low his word that he would still look out, no matter what the outcome of the case is.

Constance visited on a regular basis, hoping and praying it would be all over soon.

Todd was diligently working on the case and so far had gotten the wire taps suppressed because of the State's improper disclosure. Now, the only thing the feds had to work with was their star witness Corey Fields, better known as Cash.

"I can't believe this nigga snitching on me after all I've done for him," Real barked as he and Todd sat behind the defendants' table in the courtroom, dressed in the finest suit money could buy, waiting on Real's trial to start.

"Corey is the most crucial part of their case. I got to discredit him, which won't be too hard. The one thing they don't know that I know is that Corey was arrested with over ten kilos in a two-week time frame. I'm going to show the jury what a desperate man will do to save himself…finger his friend who's a legitimate businessman. I'm going to rip old Corey apart on the stand," Todd said with a smile.

"Man, I can't believe this nigga," Real said as he adjusted his tie.

Constance sat behind the defendants' table in the rear of the courtroom with Bible in hand, silently praying for Real. She watched intently as the trial started.

The prosecutor was way off course without the wire tap conversations. Her whole case was based solely on Cash's testimony. After Todd and the prosecutor went blow for blow, the judge told them to call their witnesses. Todd didn't have any witnesses, but the State did.

"The State calls Corey Fields to the stand," the prosecutor announced as the courtroom suddenly went quiet and Cash was brought in from the back dressed in slacks and a dress shirt.

As Cash walked across the floor, he had to pass directly in front of Real's table. He abruptly turned his head as Real made eye contact with him.

Constance watched Cash also in disbelief as he walked through the courtroom. Real had told her about the betrayal, but she never thought he would actually take the stand against Real, being that they were like family. Cash walked in a slump over up to the witness stand and took a seat behind the microphone.

"Mr. Fields, is the man in question in the room?" the prosecutor asked as she paced the floor in front of the stand.

"Yes," Cash uttered, trying his best not to look in Real's direction.

"Could you please point him out?" The prosecutor ordered as she turned to Real's direction.

Cash looked up, now having to make eye contact with Real. They met each other's glance as Cash's arm came up with finger extended directly at Real.

"Is that the man, Richard Walker, the one in the brown suit?" the prosecutor asked Cash to get a verbal confirmation for the record.

"Yes," Cash mumbled as the prosecutor started asking question after question. Before she finished, she had Real looking like a murdering, money-laundering, drug dealer who had no regard for anybody's life but his own.

Right after the prosecutor finished her tirade, Todd got up and started questioning Cash. Todd went real easy, loosening Cash up for the most important question of the day. "Mr. Fields, even though the prosecutor didn't include any records of this in the discovery, which is mandatory by law, I want to ask you myself just to make it part of the record. Did you get arrested twice—not once, but twice—with over ten kilos of cocaine in your possession both times?" Todd asked firmly as he stepped back and took in the surprised look on Cash's and the jurors' faces. Todd knew this one question alone would kill the prosecutor's whole case.

Cash sat on the stand, dumbfounded, not knowing whether to lie and perjure himself or to tell the truth. He looked over at the prosecutor, who sat at the table fiddling with some papers like she hadn't heard the question.

"Sir, do you need for me to ask you the question again? Did you or did you not get arrested? Were you not granted immunity for your bogus testimony here today?" Todd asked Cash.

After answering, "Yes," Cash was dismissed and led out of the courtroom. Cash silently prayed for a guilty verdict, because he knew Real was plotting revenge. As miserable as lockup was, he'd rather be on the inside, safe from Real if Real was found not guilty.

After wrapping up the closing arguments, Todd took a seat back at table while the jury was led from the courtroom for de-liberation.

An hour later, the jury returned.

"Now is the moment of truth," Todd said, looking over at Real, who had turned and looked back at Constance, who held her head down in silent prayer.

The jury foremen stood and spoke. "We, the jury, find Richard Walker not guilty on all counts."

Constance screamed in the back of the courtroom while Real and Todd shook hands. Just as Real was about to head over to Constance, an Atlanta policeman who had sat through the whole trial grabbed him and put him in cuffs.

"Man, hold up! What the fuck you doing?" Real yelled as Todd hurried over.

"You have an outstanding warrant for an illegal firearm that was in your possession when you were arrested," the big Black, bald-headed policeman told Real.

Constance bolted from the back of the courtroom to see what was going on.

"Real, just be easy. I'll take care of it," Todd said as the officer escorted Real outside to his patrol car.

"Baby, it's cool," Real told Constance as she followed.

A few weeks later, after vigorous litigating, Todd lost out. Real was sentenced to five years for the gun. Todd's words still rang in Real's ears, "Sometimes the small cases are harder than the bigger ones."

After sentencing, Real was shipped from Rice Street to CSSP, a diagnostic prison way down south. After going through the diagnostic process, Real was transferred to GSCP, the most dangerous prison in the State of Georgia.

After the federal trial, Cash was given immunity and released. After lying low for a while, he set up shop again in the city of Macon.

Back in Atlanta, Constance filed paperwork on Real's behalf to get their property back while she worked vigorously to build up her newly established realtor business.

B-Low was steadily taking over the streets of Atlanta. With the money Real fronted him, he traveled down to Jacksonville, Florida, to shop for some work and met Juan, the son of Pablo, one of the South's biggest drug suppliers.

While everybody was trying to get back on track in Real's absence, Real was steadily trying to stay alive in GSCP, where two gangs were trying to earn the half-million-dollar bounty that the Italians were offering for his death.

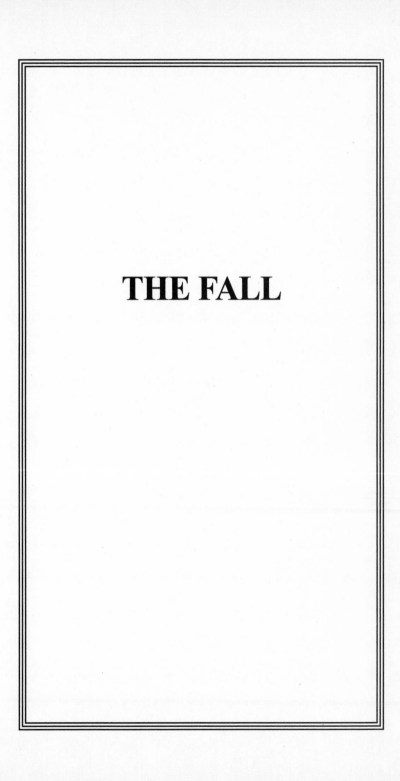

THE FALL

Chapter 31

" *Y*eah right there! Oh shit, suck that dick! Oh fuck I…
I'm about to…"

"Blam! Blam!" The gun rang out in the expensively furnished luxury condo, splitting the head of Red- one of Macon, Georgia's biggest drug dealers.

"Nigga, you got to close!" Lace screamed at Cash, who quickly tucked the glock 40 in his waist and started searching the condo for Red's stash.

"Bitch quit tripping and just help me find this loot!" Cash screamed as he turned over the custom made furniture in his search.

Cash and Lace were on a mission to get rich whatever the cost. Cash met Lace three months ago at Club Erotica one of Macon's most popular strip clubs. After realizing they were both from Atlanta and both on the grind to come up, they exchanged numbers.

Cash knew he desperately needed someone down for the cause since he was in a new city and unfamiliar territory. Lace was just what Cash was looking for because she was down for the come up and just like himself, he knew Lace would kill with no questions asked.

Having been released by the feds after his testimony in Real's trial; Cash relocated to Macon because he knew before long niggas all over the city of Atlanta would be gunning for him for being a snitch. While sitting in jail waiting to testify on Real, his house was foreclosed on and his Benz was repossessed, all he had was his hooptie, three thousand dollars, his 9mm and a plan to come up. After being released he packed what he had left and headed down south to Macon with plans to get back on top.

"Where the fuck this nigga keep the money," Lace called out as she went from room to room searching.

Lace was the true definition of a gangsta bitch. On top of that she was one of the baddest bitches out of Atlanta. Her small waist, wide hips and big ass like Buffy the Body had not just men but also women pushing up on her. Sipping on a glass of Hennessy in Club Erotica one night, Cash spotted the green eyed Lace from across the club as her bow legs and thick thighs jiggled to the sound of Rick Ross blasting from the club sound system. He walked over and introduced himself. Since that night they've been plotting and scheming on every kind of hustle imaginable.

Cash really wasn't Lace's type but after finding out he was from Atlanta and out to get paid by whatever means necessary, she became totally interested. Lace was down and out also and the money she made in the club wasn't enough for her to maintain her diva lifestyle. After listening to Cash's plans to come up, she knew if she got down with him she would most definitely get paid; besides, she saw herself in Cash, a heartless hustler down for getting money by any means necessary, even if it called for murder.

"Bingo!" Cash screamed from the back bedroom.

"Shit!" Lace screamed as she stepped in the room where Cash was and saw the overturned mattress filled with tightly wrapped stacks of money.

"This nigga wasn't bullshitting! Let's pack this shit and get up out of here," Cash said as he started pulling the wads of money out of the gutted out mattress.

Lace and Cash packed the money up and discreetly exited

Red's condo locking the door behind them.

"That's what I'm talking 'bout! Give this boss bitch a kiss," Lace said as she leaned over to Cash who was behind the wheel of the old Lebaron.

"Bitch back up didn't you just get a dick out ya mouth! You trying me," Cash snapped.

"Damn! I'm sorry I fuckin' forgot and you know I ain't trying you," Lace replied, knowing Cash wasn't to be tested in no kind of way, not if you wanted to live.

They rode through Macon in silence back out to Lace's apartment near Popular Street. The whole ride home Lace stared out the window and plotted on a way to kill Cash so she could keep all the money. Little did she know that Cash had the same thoughts as he navigated the old beat up Lebaron through the back streets of Macon.

" $\mathcal{Y}$ ou have a collect call from…Real…an inmate in a Georgia State Correctional Facility if you accept press five, if you…"

Constance smiled as she waited for the operator to patch Real in.

"Hey boo what's going on?" Real asked as he put his back against the wall while talking staying fully aware of his surroundings.

Real had been at GSCP now for a couple of months. New to the prison system, Real knew he had to adjust and fast. Real met Tino, from Atlanta, who gave him the run down on prison living. After hearing the men out Real couldn't believe how you had to live on the inside just to survive.

"Nothing much just missing the hell out of you," Constance said as she looked out of her office window at the men and women downtown rushing back and forth to their destinations.

Constance started her own real estate firm soon after Real was sent off to prison. She purchased some exclusive office space downtown from one of her broker friends and set up her a property database. Already having a long list of potential wealthy clients made it real easy for her, she was pulling in major cash in her first week of business. Just last week she sold Antoine

Vernon—the starting safety for the Atlanta Falcons a 2.6 million dollar home out in the Buckhead area, in which she made a generous commission.

"Miss you too! What's been going on? Has B-low been keeping in touch?"

"Yeah he came by the office yesterday, he told me to tell you everything is going good and to call him."

"Ok good. How's my boo been doing? I got the approval papers back for visitation, you can come down Saturday and Sunday from nine to three. Oh and in a couple of days I should have a cell phone. I'm going to need you to Money Gram three hundred for me."

"Ok just let me know," Constance replied.

"Baby this shit is crazy! Niggas having sex with the female guards, selling dope like they on the corner, and everybody got a cell phone," Real said, still tripping at how niggas was living in prison.

"You got to be kidding! They doing all that? Where the guards at? Oh I forgot, you said they getting they groove on. That's a crazy place," Constance said, shocked at Real's description of the living conditions in prison.

"One dude got his face sliced up over the TV last night. Dude wanted to watch the news on the sports TV so he got up and turned the TV while some lil crazy nigga was watching Sport Center. A few minutes later dude busted out of the TV room holding his face with his hands full of blood. The other lil nigga busted out behind him and chased him with the blade around the dorm until the guards came. These niggas crazy!"

"Baby you just be careful. Please be careful," Constance said softly as her eyes watered.

"Baby you know I'm going to hold it down, I just want you to keep stacking that paper. By the way what's up with our cars and house? What did Todd say they talking about?" Real asked, as he watched two young gang bangers rap and throw up gang signs as they watched B.E.T. .

"I faxed him the paperwork he needed last week, they should be releasing everything by the end of the month. The club is a different story you may be mad at me but I thought it would be best to just let it go," Constance said hoping Real would understand.

"That's cool really, I think we should just sell everything and start over anyway. As soon as they release everything start selling it and banking the money. We going to see about relocating when I come home. We need a long vacation so we can start working on poking that stomach out," Real laughed.

"Whatever boy, you crazy! It would be nice though, just think…"

"You have fifteen seconds," the automated voice chimed in.

"Dang! Call me back," Constance said before the phone could hang up.

"O…" Real started just as the call was disconnected.

Real made sure the line was clear and then started dialing Constance number again.

"Hold up my nigga, you got folks in line trying to holla at their people too!" The tall dark skin brother with a body full of indescript tattoos screamed as he walked up on Real.

"Bro I ain't see nobody waiting, that other phone over there is open anyway," Real replied, not looking for a confrontation.

"Naw my nigga I want this phone so you need to be hanging it up!" The tall brother said as spit flew out his mouth into Real's face.

Real did everything he could to keep his cool but when the spit hit his lip, he snapped. Before the tall brother could react Real had two pieced him sending him backwards into the table. Not giving him a chance to recover. Real was on top of him smashing his face with his fist. Out of nowhere Real was hit on the shoulder with a lock tied on a belt.

"Fuck!" Real said, trying to get out of the way from the heavy set brother swinging the lock at him.

Real backed up to the wall as both the men started in his

direction. Just as they got in arms length, Real fired again, this time on the brother with the lock. Real knew he was doomed if he didn't get away. Seeing the commotion in the front of the dorm, Tino made his way to the front. Seeing Real fighting his heart out Tino jumped in. Tino was known throughout the prison for his hand work. Going hard on the tall brother, it didn't take Tino long to knock him out. Real seeing Tino putting in work on his behalf was relieved. Now focusing, he squared off with the heavy set brother with the lock. Real stepped to him throwing a swift uppercut followed by a knee to his nut sack. The brother doubled over in pain. Real stepped back and free styled on the brother hitting him from every angle with ease. Before the guards rushed the building it was over. Ms. Whales the floor officer was too busy giving her boyfriend Flint some head to know what was going on. Real and Tino hurried back to Tino room before they were caught.

"Man what the fuck wrong with them niggas?" Real asked Tino out of breath.

"Niggas gonna try you just to see what you are made of. That nigga Slim Shady always pulling up on niggas with the bullshit. They see you get down for yours now so it's all good," Tino told Real as he peeked out the door at Ms. Whales trying to find out what went on.

"Damn!" Real spat as he sat on Tino's bottom bunk holding his hand.

"You ain't seen nothing yet. Welcome to jungle."

Chapter 33

" *I* want him dead! I don't care where he is!" Angelo
screamed into the phone to his lieutenant.

"I have a couple of people on the inside that I'll contact. I'm
pretty sure they can handle it," Michael told Angelo as he pushed
the old model Mercedes Benz through downtown Miami.

"Good just let them know we paying a half million to have
him eliminated," Angelo said firmly thinking back on the day
Real killed his uncle.

"I will contact them now. I will call you back this evening,"
Michael replied ending the call.

Hanging up with Michael, Angelo clicked over and dialed
Milo's number.

"Hello?" Milo answered.

"Milo I need you to bring over the two hundred fifty thousand
for the bounty on Real, I have my people making contact to get
him taken care of right now. They have located him in a down
south Georgia prison," Angelo said with disdain in his voice not
liking the man on the line.

Milo and Angelo were nephews of two of the richest and
deadliest men in the cartel. After Real waged war and killed
both of their uncles they came together to get revenge for the
murders. Even though they were working together to get revenge,

Angelo still hated Milo with a passion for his renegade ways and arrogance. Both men were sworn in to lead their family after their uncles were murdered.

"Good, I will have my driver deliver the money this afternoon. Keep me updated. What is the status on his girlfriend?"

"She will be taken care of also," Angelo confirmed

"I'll be in touch," Milo replied then hung up.

Angelo put another call in to Blanco his highly paid assassin. Blanco stood five foot even and weighed only one hundred and twenty pounds. Blanco was small but a very dangerous man; deadly as they come. Blanco was paid to find Constance and take her out. Blanco drove up to Atlanta and located Constance in a matter of days now he was patiently waiting until the time was right to end her existence. Blanco loved the thrill of the kill more than the money he was paid.

"Talk to me," Blanco answered .

"What's the status on the girl?" Angelo asked hoping he had found her by now.

"I have her in my sights all I have to do now is pull the trigger! Pow! Pow! Pow! Baka! Baka! Baka!" Blanco screamed out crazily.

"That's good my friend. Let me know when it's taken care of," Angelo told him and hurried off the phone with the crazy, deranged killer.

Chapter 34

"Damn my nigga, how just last week you charge me seventeen five and now you talking twenty even," JP one of B-low's many customers spat.

"Say bro, who selling this shit! You putting prices on my shit now? You want it or not, shit you acting like you copping ten or better," B-low told JP as they sat out in B-low's Yukon in front of JP's apartment.

"Damn bro, fuck with your boy, I got eighteen right now you know it get greater later," JP replied as he sat the bag of money on the middle console.

"Twenty straight up and down you wasting my time and time is money!" B-low snapped.

"That's fucked up bro, but this my last time at this tag," JP said as he pulled two more thousand from his pocket.

"Good business holla back," B-low told JP as he exited the truck with the brick of cocaine tucked under his arm.

B-low was the go to man in the city now. Taking the money Real fronted down to Jacksonville he shopped around for a good deal on some work. Through one of his connects he met Juan the son of Pablo one of the south's biggest dealers. Juan was trying to expand his operation when he pulled B-low in and presented him a deal. The deal was for every brick bought he would front him one. That's not what really reeled B-low in though. What really hooked B-low was the price of ten flat. Every since then B-low have been taking over the city block by block. No one in the city could compete with his prices.

B-low had become a seven figure nigga in no time. He had purchased him a half a million dollar home in Gwinnett, two luxury cars, and was working on starting his own construction company. B-low supplied damn near the whole south Georgia, if not directly it was through one of his many workers that he had positioned in each city. B-low took the game to a level he never thought he could reach; he was determined to take over the south.

B-low knew he owed all his success to Real so that's why every time he made a play he put a couple G's to the side for Real. B-low also made sure that Constance didn't want for anything while Real was down. He promised Real that he would look after her until he came home. Over the short period of time, he and Constance had become good friends. Constance looked at him like a big brother.

Every day B-low was out hustling he thought about Jesse-his partner, who'd been shot and the day that he had to leave him behind, while trying to get away from the gang of Italians who was gunning for him and Real after they took out the head of one of their families. He missed his partner, they had dreams to live the life that he was now living. To this day, he never knew what happened to his friend. He hated that Jesse didn't even get a proper burial. B-low thought about the Italians and revenge daily.

Heading out to the gym he looked down at his vibrating cell phone. It was Kasi a lil chocolate dance instructor from Riverdale. He didn't answer, he'd missed the gym two days in a row. He knew if he wanted to keep his six three, two hundred forty pounds in shape he would have to stay consistent. Since his new found wealth and new look he's been told he favored his favorite wide receiver, T.O., in which he took in stride because just last year this time he was just an unknown jack boy from the Westside. His life had taken a three sixty since then and he loved it.

Chapter 35

$\mathcal{T}$he next morning Real and Tino stayed close just in case the fight last night carried over in to the day. The two men from last night was absent from breakfast which they never missed. Real and Tino sat together in the chow hall watching each other's back while discussing the suspicious absence of the two men this morning at breakfast.

"You got that tool I gave you?" Tino asked Real as they kept a close eye out for the men from last night.

"Naw, I left it in the heater," Real replied looking over Tino's shoulder at the chow hall door every time it opened.

"In the heater! Bro you got to stay strapped at all times! When you sleep, eat, shit, shower, man you got to stay strapped!" Tino said firmly as he adjusted the shank he carried in his front pocket.

"I ain't think tha…"

"At all times bro! You at war everyday! You never know when shit going to pop off, so it's better to be safe than sorry," Tino said, as two older inmates sat down at their table.

"I feel you," Real replied as he finished off the rest of his oatmeal.

Leaving the chow hall headed back to the dorm, Real and Tino noticed a group of gang bangers standing out by the laundry entrance. Real didn't notice the threat but Tino picked right up on it.

"Say bro make sure your boots tied tight shit ain't looking right," Tino whispered to Real as the approached the crowd of gang bangers.

"Yo G, you Real? The muscle bound young banger asked Real as he stepped out in front of Real blocking his way."

Real was no coward he walked up and got directly in the bangers face ready for whatever. Looking around sizing the men up he positioned himself for a solid swing. Tino had pulled the shank from his pocket and concealed it in the sleeve of his jacket. Tino surveyed the crowd even though they were out-numbered, he knew they had a good chance to take the bangers especially if Real put on a performance like the one he put on last night.

"Yeah I'm Real what up?" Real asked standing his ground.

"The name Sandman ring a bell?" the banger asked.

Real didn't recognize the name off the top, then he remembered the only Sandman he knew. That Sandman had been shot and killed years ago by the police, and Real paid for the funeral with his re-up money. Real and Sandman had grew up together out on Godby Road in College Park, they were like brothers. His mom Jackie always treated Real like her own. After leaving the hood Real lost touch with Ms. Jackie, last he heard, her and lil BayBay Sandman's little brother had moved out to Fairburn Georgia.

"Yeah I know a Sandman. Why? What's up?" Real asked this time about to swing fed up with the questions.

"You sure?" the banger asked. "Where he from?"

"College Park, Godby Road. Man move out my way with all these questions," Real said, getting frustrated.

"You are Real! Bro this BayBay," the banger said excitedly.

"BayBay? Hell naw!"Real screamed.

"Yeah man I was a lil boy last time you seen me, I was out around the hood on my bike."

"Muthafuckin BayBay," Real said as him and the banger

embraced.

Tino was relieved, it was way too cold and too early to be rumbling. He quietly slid the shank back in his pocket. The other bangers looked on as Real and their leader BayBay chopped it up about the past.

"Bro, how mama been doing? What the hell you locked up for?" Real asked happy to see BayBay.

"Man mama died last year, she had a heart attack while working. It's been hard bro, my baby worked herself to death," BayBay said faintly.

"Damn bro, I'm sorry to hear that. How long have you been gone?"

"Goin on six years now. I caught a body case down in Dublin, Ga. A country nigga flexed my folks for ten of them thangs. They hit me up and broke me off to see bout the nigga. Went to the nigga house laid him down and dome called him and his bitch. Bro I got away clean but I made the mistake and told my girl, as soon as she caught me down bad with her friend she screamed on me now I'm sitting in this bitch with two life's and thirty," BayBay explained as Tino and the other bangers listened in.

"Damn lil bro it ain't over, when I get up out of here I'll help you," Real said thanking God for his five years.

"I appreciate it bro I knew when they told me a nigga with crazy colored eyes from College Park named Real and a nigga named Tino had went to work on some niggas, I knew it had to be you. That's your people?" BayBay asked looking over at Tino.

"Yeah this Tino; hey Tino this my lil big homey BayBay." Real introduced them.

"I done heard of playa. YouTino with the nice hand game that like to play with them tools?" BayBay asked

"I don't play wit em," Tino said in a firm tone.

"I hear you bro yall…"

"Hey all yall get to your building! Move on or go to lock up!" Sergeant Blake screamed from across the yard.

"I'll get at yall later, let's go before this nigga call the cert team," BayBay said as him and his soldiers eased off to their building.

Chapter 36

" *T*his nigga got me fucked up if he think he just giving me twelve thousand and he keeping over ninety thousand," Lace mumbled to herself as she looked at Cash who laid in the bed sleep.

Thoughts of picking up his glock off the nightstand and unloading it in him crossed her mind. After quickly dismissing the thought she walked on her toes quietly across the room to the closet where he had stashed the money. Opening the door while peeping back at him she lifted the bag just enough to unzip it and grabbed a handful of bills. After getting a nice size bundle of bills she zipped the bag back up and put it back in the position she found it. Easing the closet back up she looked over at Cash to make sure he was still sleep.

Cash watched Lace out one eye as she stole money from the bag in the closet. Cash really just wanted to jump up and beat her down real bad but decided against it after thinking about his next move the one that he really needed her help with. After watching her ease back to the other side of the room Cash lifted his head.

"What time is it baby?" Cashed asked groggily faking sleep.

"Oh it's almost twelve," Lace answered innocently as she combed her hair.

Lace and Cash was an odd couple like night and day. The one

thing that the both of them knew but never voiced was that their relations were strictly based on the money, the come up and the next lick. Lace had a plan to get hers through Cash or from Cash. Cash on the same note was tired of Lace bitching about her cut and how much he stacking so he made up his mind after this last lick, Lace was history.

Cash got up and got dressed while Lace cleaned the apartment. After getting dressed he grabbed the bag of money from the closet and told Lace he would be back.

Exiting the apartment he got in the Lebaron and headed out to Tenet Homes to holla at Milk Man, the go to man that he met when he first arrived in town. Milk Man had the connect, he told Cash when he was ready to shop he would give him the work for nineteen a block way more than the ten and twelve him and Real use to get them for. Cash agreed on the price only because after the second meeting he was going to up the order and take Milk Man for the whole bag anyway.

Lace's cell phone rang as Cash was leaving the apartment.

"I don't know when he's coming back, just hold off until tomorrow it will be way more money then," Lace told her baby daddy—Black Bean on the other line, who sat on his old ripped up couch in his trap house on the west side of Atlanta.

"Why wait I can be out there tonight! You acting like you trying to be with this nigga! Who is this nigga anyway?" Black Bean asked getting heated.

Lace and Black Bean had been on bad terms when she met Cash but after a visit to Atlanta and a wild night of sex they had put their differences aside. Black Bean knew how Lace played the game and when she told him about the nigga she met that was putting down the pistol and stacking nice numbers they came up with a plan. The plan was to let Cash go hit all the licks with her help and afterwards they would take him for all the dough.

"Boy you know better! Me and you been together way to long for you to be coming at me like that! Just be patient until tomorrow! Matter of fact just come on and get a room so when the time right you will be close and the nigga name is Cash, he from Atlanta," Lace said snappy.

"Cash? I know a nigga name Cash. What he look like?" Black Bean inquired.

"He's a tall, red nigga with a dollar sign tattooed under his eye. He…"

"Snitch, bitch ass nigga! That's the nigga that told on B-low's partner Real! That's the nigga from the south side that was putting down big work! This nigga robbing now? Oh he know he can't step foot back in the city! Man this police ass nigga! I'm coming out tonight!" Black Bean said firmly while rolling up a blunt of purp.

"This that nigga B-low was talking 'bout?" Lace asked disgusted, she hated a snitch ass nigga.

"Yep, the one and only."

"Daaaammmmnn! All this time I thought he was certified," Lace said in disbelief.

"It's hard to tell a real nigga from a fake these days, I'll holla when I get there," Black Bean said as he hung up the phone.

Chapter 37

Constance grabbed her purse, exited her office and headed down to her favorite lunch spot after going over her list of multimillion dollar properties that were up for sale. Blanco sat in his late model Chevy Blazer and watched as she got in her Bentley and made a left out of the parking lot.

Blanco had decided to make his move today. He watched her long enough now to know her schedule. Stepping out of the Blazer he made his way up to the office door. Looking around making sure the coast was clear he wedged his screwdriver in between the door jam and a second later the office door popped open.

"Hooray!" A mentally challenged Blanco said excitedly to himself, as he stepped into the expensively furnished office and found a comfortable place to sit and relax while he waited for Constance to return.

Constance smelled the onion rings and chilli dogs as she pulled up into the Varsity parking lot. Constance really wanted to enjoy this time away from the office but she knew she couldn't. Having to take care of the closing on a newly acquired property, she knew that if she wanted to be out of the office by six she would have to skip the dining in and just grab her order to go.

While waiting on her order Constance constantly checked her cell phone to make sure that she hadn't missed a call from Real.

She even dialed her own number to make sure that the phone was transferred properly. Last night after hanging up with Real she stayed close to the phone hoping that he would call right back. Constance missed the hell out of Real. She counted down the days til his release. All she thought about was him and how they were going to get married and start a family when he came home. The old black grey haired man holding her bag of food jarred her out of her deep thought.

"Hi, ma'am, that'll be seven twenty."

Paying for her order and tipping the old man generously Constance headed back to her office to finalize the closing.

Blanco sat in her office desk chair and flipped through the papers on her desk while he waited for her to return. After sitting around for about 30 minutes he heard a car out front. Peeping out of the blinds he saw that it was Constance. He watched her through the blinds up until she was out of his sight and at the door. He put his back against the wall behind the door and pulled out his hunting knife.

Constance exited the car and rushed up to the door with her bag of food in hand. She fumbled with her keys until she found the office door key. Blanco tightened his grip on the knife as Constance was about to enter.

Chapter 38

" Why the fuck you calling telling me, all I know is you owe me twenty six and a half and I want every penny," B-low spat as he pushed his brand new Rolls Royce Ghost down Flat Shoals in route to the Kawasaki dealership out on Riverdale road.

"Bro this nigga just ran off with a hundred bands! Just give me a minute and I'll be right back at you with that and some extra," Toin lied as he sat at his kitchen table counting his weekly profits.

Toin was one of B-low's best workers. He would turn in no less than fifty thousand a week. Toin was loyal up until he met Rain Man—a Jamaican who hand a firm hold on the Miami drug trade. Toin took the money he owed B-low and spent it with Rain Man on a deal he couldn't refuse. Toin knew he could flip the money in a week's time but he wasn't expecting a delay in the second part of the shipment.

Toin sat at the table counted the money and did the math. He knew if he paid B-low out of his weekly profits he would fall way behind while he waited for the second half of the shipment so he decided to hold off until the next part of the shipment arrived.

"Look here people, I ain't got nothing to do with what you let a nigga do! I am sending someone for my money at four. If you ain't got my money we are going to have some serious problems!" B-low barked as he clicked Toin off the line and called Hulk, his personal bodyguard and hitman.

"Say Hulk, I got a problem, I need you to go holla at Toin at four and if he ain't got my twenty six and a half beat him til he come up with it!"

"Toin? The frog looking dude who stay out in East Point?" Hulk asked

"Yeah, the one with the chevy with the big wheels. Holla at shawty at four and if he ain't got that bread, punish him good," B-low instructed Hulk, who would follow his commands without hesitation.

Hulk was B-low's muscle not that B-low wasn't built to handle his own but he knew he was at a level in the game now where you didn't get your hands dirty unless you had no other choice. After frequent visits to Strokers, B-low convinced Hulk who was the head of the security to work for him for double the pay. Hulk didn't hesitate to become part of B-low's team. B-low was glad to have the six foot four, three hundred pound special opts trained man on his team.

"I got you I'll call you with an update later," Hulk replied as they ended the call.

Pulling up into the Kawasaki dealership lot B-low spotted what he was looking for before he even got out the car. The all black Kawasaki Ninja ZX-14 was parked up front in the display window. B-low parked the Ghost and entered the shop.

"Hi. Could you have that bike right there delivered to this address?" B-low asked the young Chinese salesman as he handed him a business card.

"The ZX-14—good choice! How do you pay? Ten percent down with credit check," the salesman said in broken English.

"Cash," B-low said as he unzipped his small Gucci handbag that contained fifteen thousand dollars in brand new one hundred dollar bills.

"Okay. Come right over here," he excitedly told B-low, thinking about the hefty comission he was about to make.

After purchasing the bike B-low headed downtown to see about Constance, who he made it his business to check on every week. He gave Real his word to look out for Constance while he was away and planned to stand by it. It didn't take him long to get to her office. As he was pulling up in the parking lot he spotted her clumsily trying to get in her office door with a bag of food in her hand.

"Hey lady you need some help!" B-low screamed from the car window as he parked.

Blanco who stood quietly behind the door heard another voice outside. Quickly peeping out of the window he saw a man getting out his car walking up to the door where Constance stood trying to open the door.

"Shit!" Blanco cursed, knowing his job had just got harder.

With only one way out he knew he was going to have to confront both of them. He eased back over behind the door with his hunting knife in hand.

"Hey B-low! Real been trying to catch up with you," Constance told him as he walked over to her at the office door.

"Why he ain't called? I need to holla at bro. Next time he call see if he need me to handle anything and tell him to hit me at the 678 number. How you doing? You ok? Need anything?" B-low asked Constance while he descreetly looked at her from head to toe.

"No, I'm fine just got a lot of work to do," Constance said as she opened the door and stepped in with B-low following.

As soon as B-low closed the door he looked in the eyes of a deranged Blanco who pounced on him immediately with the hunting knife.

"What the…"

Constance turned when she heard B-low yell. She instantly went in attack mode seeing the man stabbing at B-low with the big sharp blade.

"Get the fuck out of here!" Constance yelled as she picked up the vase off her desk and swung it, hitting the knife, wielding man square in the face.

"Oh, fuck!" Blanco screamed as the blood trickled from his head.

B-low took that moment to grab the little man. Securing his grip he swung wildly connecting with Blanco time and time again. Blanco realized that he wasn't going to succeed in taking out his target so he did what he rarely ever did, he ran. He bolted for the door as Constance and B-low continued their assault. Blanco looked back as he ran towards the Blazer. Seeing that there was no one following he jumped in, started the engine and burned rubber out of the parking lot.

"What in the hell was that all about! I'm calling 911 and an ambulance you bleeding like crazy!" Constance said as she helped B-low over to her office lounger.

"Naw don't call the police I'm cool just a flesh wound. What in the hell was…it had to be a hit on you," B-low declared as he moaned out in pain from the cut on his shoulder.

"Hit? From who?" Constance asked faintly becoming nervous.

"The Italians! That little bitch was an Italian! They more than likely are after revenge for the murders! Arggghh," B-low said in pain.

"Murders? What murders?" Constance asked getting hysterical.

"Nothing we just got to get you out of here and keep you safe," B-low explained.

"I ain't goin nowhere til I find out what's going on!" Constance yelled.

"I don't know if I am suppose to be telling you this but, to make a long story short Real killed some men for kidnapping you now they out for revenge."

Chapter 39

" *O*ne, two, three, four…" Real huffed and puffed as he did his daily set of push-ups.

"Damn my nigga, you could have screamed at a nigga I would have got down with you," the three hundred pound KP said playfully, as he stood over Real doing push-ups.

"Yeah right nigga. Man what's up with the flops?" Real asked getting up anxiously, waiting for KP to make his next drop of cell phones.

"Shawty suppose to be bringing them tomorrow. You know you first on the list," KP assured Real as he pushed on by Real who had got down for his next set.

Real had become popular real quick around GSCP. After the beating he put on Slim Shady the other inmates saw that he was a rider then his affiliation with BayBay let everybody know he had a real killer on his team. Him and Tino had become real tight after the brawl. Real gave Tino his word that he would look out for him when he got out. Real felt bad for Tino being that he had life without parole and would never see the streets again. Tino had killed an off duty police eight years ago while trying to car jack him. Real knew Tino regretted the day he flagged the man down and then took his life just to get his set of rims and stereo system.

"Stand by for inspection! Stand by for inspection!" The young, under-weight, blond hair, blue eyed Mrs. Reynolds yelled across the dorm.

Inspection was the worst part of the day for most of the inmates at GSCP. They hated having to stand by their room door fully dressed in their prison uniform at attention in the hot summer heat while their rooms were inspected by the Warden, CERT team and other prison officials.

"Fuck! This muthafucka don't miss a day!" Real spat to himself referring to Mr. Grant- the prison warden.

Real hurried to his room to get ready. All across the dorm men were tucking in their shirts, hiding contraband, drinking cups of water just in case they were piss testing and straightening their cells. Real put on his shirt, checked the heater to make sure his shank was well hid and stood outside his door and waited for the inspection team to reach the building.

"Coming cross the yard!" someone yelled from the front of the dorm.

Everyone positioned themselves outside of their door as Mrs. Reynolds pressed the button to open the front door to let the warden in. The balding, pale, in bad need of a tan, Warden Grant lead the pack with the CERT team, captain, lieutenant, two seargents, and head counselor following.

"Warden on deck!" the dorm rep yelled from the front of the dorm.

"Sir, good morning sir!" all the inmates screamed in unison as the inspection team stood in the middle of the dorm floor.

"I can't hear you!" the warden yelled positioning his hands behind his ears.

"Sir! Good morning! Sir!" the men yelled again this time much louder.

"That's better," The warden said as he called all his staff together for a huddle.

As soon as they broke up their huddle the CERT team and all the other officers started at each end of the dorm closing all the room doors.

"Everybody line up, place your hands on top of your head and face the wall! Anybody that can't follow directions will go to lockdown! First man head to the gym!" the warden screamed.

It was a shakedown.

Chapter 40

"   *W*here you at?" Lace asked BlackBean as she sat on her tattered leather couch watching Forensic Files on her flat screen TV.

"I should be reaching the exit in about 45 minutes. I'm going to get me a room at the Super 8 right off the expressway, what time the nigga coming back to your spot?" Black Bean asked as he came up on his exit.

"He probably will be back around ten, but like I said we need to wait til tomorrow after we hit this lick out in Tenant Homes that way it will be more money," Lace explained.

"Fuck that, I'm going to get this nigga tonight! Just leave the door unlocked when yall go to bed tonight,"Black Bean ordered.

"I'm trying to tell you, we…"

Black Bean snapped.

"Look just leave the fuckin door unlocked tonight!"

"Fine then! Fuck it!" Lace fired back.

While Black Bean and Lace were plotting Cash was headed back to the apartment with four bricks and a lil over ten thousand left in his bag. Cash couldn't wait to get back into the swing of things in this city waiting to be taken. Cash counted the profits in his head while he pushed the raggedy Lebaron down the city streets back to the apartment. Tomorrow he would call Milkman back to meet him with four more blocks for his partner from the A. That would be their last meeting and Milkman last day breathing.

Cash pulled up grabbed his bag with the cocaine and money and headed up to the door. As he reached the door he heard Lace talking to somebody on the phone. Cash stooped down and slid over to the open screened in window that was right in front of the couch that Lace sat on and listened.

"I ain't tripping you need to wait so we can get more money you rushing and shit! I'm telling you this nigga going to hit another lick tomorrow! Why not wait til then and get everything!" Lace yelled.

Cash stood silently and listened.

"Fuck it then I'll just leave the door open tonight, bye!" Lace screamed and hung up the phone.

Cash backed away from the window with bag in hand and used his key to open the door.

"Baby what's up? Where you been?" Lace called out as Cash entered, seeing him in a different light after finding out he was a snitch.

"Trying to set this play up for tomorrow. After this play, ain't no looking back. What's up with you?" Cash asked as he sat down next to Lace on the couch.

"Shit, chilling just thinking," Lace said laying her head on Cash shoulder.

"What you thinking about?" Cash asked playing along.

"Me and you. I want us to make this last lick and kick back. I want us to go on a long vacation and when we get back I want us to buy a nice house and just enjoy each other," Lace lied really thinking about Black Bean and the lick tonight while kissing Cash on the neck.

"That sounds good to me. After tomorrow we will be able to live easy. I got a plan to touch every piece of dope money that come through the city. I'm going to take this bitch over," Cash said with enthusiasm really enjoying Lace kisses on his neck knowing she was going to be dead by morning.

"I can't wait," Lace said as she rubbed her hand in between his legs gripping his dick.

"Me either," Cash said as he laid back and let Lace hands and mouth roam.

Cash carefully went over his plans in his head. He knew more than likely the person on the other end of the phone would be at the apartment after dark. Cash smiled at the thought of the punishment he would inflict on Lace and her conspirator. Cash laid back as Lace pulled his dick out his pants and started sucking.

Chapter 41

"*I* can't believe this! I need to talk to Real!" Constance barked as her and B-low exited her office.

"Look, everything is cool but you going to have to close down this place and move out your spot because more than likely they know where you lay your head. Ah fuck!" B-low yelled out trying his best to deal with the pain from the knife wound.

"I just moved! I ain't about…"

B-low cut in.

"You coming with me, I promised Real that I would keep you safe and that's what I am going to do," B-low said firmly.

"I…"

"Follow me," B-low instructed as he hurried to his car holding his bleeding wound.

Constance didn't argue she knew her life was in danger. She looked down at her cell phone hoping Real would call as she followed B-low out to Gwinnett. Constance did a double take as they pulled up in front of B-low's million dollar home. The house is not what impressed her, it was B-low financial situation. She never would have thought that even after looking at his luxury car that B-low was living a millionaire lifestyle. She guided her Bentley in behind him and parked.

"Nice house," Constance said as she helped B-low nurse his

wound as they headed up to the front door.

"Thanks," B-low said enjoying Constance touch.

Opening the front door Constance was taken in by the custom designed marble floors and all the black and gold furniture fixtures. The custom made furnishings with gold accents gave the house a feel of royalty. B-low had personally picked one of the most expensive, well know interior designers to decorate the house, giving her an unlimited budget to capture the feel he was looking for.

"Tell me what's going on. What have you and Real done to make someone want to come after me?" Constance asked with a slight hint of panic in her voice.

"I think you should holla at Real about that. Until then I want you to stay in my guest house. You need to close down your office and I will get your stuff moved into storage tomorrow. Straight up, you have to stay here because the people we are dealing with are not to be taken lightly," B-low said standing in the kitchen while placing an alcohol soaked rag on his wound.

"I want you to tell me what's going on," Constance asked again as her eyes started to water.

"Sorry can't," B-low said looking down intently into Constance big pretty eyes wanting to take her into his arms and console her.

"Why!" Constance screamed getting angry.

"As soon as I clean up we going out to your place to get your things," B-low replied ignoring her question, making Constance angry.

"You already told me that yall killed somebody! Why are they coming after me!" Constance yelled.

"Look here, we killed some Italian muthafuckas point blank period! The men we killed were heads of two of the most powerful families in the cartel. Somehow they must have found out we were behind the murders and now they out for revenge. You are just going to have to lay low until we straighten this shit out." B-low said firmly as he bandaged his wound.

MICHIGAN POWERBALL
POWERPLAY

SATURDAY'S POWERBALL JACKPOT
IS $478,000,000!
HERE'S YOUR CHANCE. BUY YOUR
POWERBALL TICKETS TODAY!

A. 11 35 44 46 55 EP   PWR 18 EP

SAT JUL30 16 $2.00
    PRINTED JUL30 16 07:25:26
    011450   10788200

1180-012056069-127219

290123252

**PLEASE CHECK TICKET FOR CORRECT
DRAWING DATE(S), NUMBER(S) AND AMOUNT**

RULES

THIS TICKET IS VALID ONLY FOR THE DRAWING DATE(S) PRINTED ON THE FRONT

All tickets, transactions and claims are subject to the laws of the State of Michigan, the rules, regulations, and all directives of the Michigan Lottery, and any changes thereto.

KEEP ALL WINNING TICKETS IN A SAFE PLACE. ALL PRIZES MUST BE CLAIMED WITHIN ONE YEAR OF DRAWING DATE. ANY CLAIM FOR A PRIZE MUST BE ACCOMPANIED BY AN AUTHENTIC WINNING TICKET WHICH IS CAPABLE OF BEING VALIDATED.

Winning tickets may be presented to an authorized Lottery retailer or any official Lottery office. Tickets which are illegible, altered, counterfeit, defective, unregistered, or which fail any part of the Lottery's validation tests are ineligible for prize payment.

Play Online at MichiganLottery.com for more chances to win cash instantly! Plus, earn Reward Points redeemable for entries in the Play It Again Giveaway when you play online and enter non-winning tickets.

> **If you bet more than you can afford to lose, you've got a problem.
> Call 1-800-270-7117 for confidential help.**

Signature of Claimant _____

THE MICHIGAN LOTTERY SUPPORTS EDUCATION.

For drawing results, call the Michigan Lottery Link 1-800-822-8888 (Toll Free),
or visit the Michigan Lottery Website at: www.michiganlottery.com

Made
in
Michigan

290123253

**PLEASE CHECK TICKET FOR CORRECT
DRAWING DATE(S), NUMBER(S) AND AMOUNT**

MICHIGAN

Fantasy 5
+ EZmatch

SATURDAY'S POWERBALL JACKPOT
IS $478,000,000!
HERE'S YOUR CHANCE. BUY YOUR
POWERBALL TICKETS TODAY!

A 01 02 11 30 36 EP

SAT JUL30 16 $1.00
      PRINTED JUL30 16 07:25:18
      014881   10788200

1180-038530305-119219

michiganlottery.com

Reward Points redeemable for entries in the Play It Again Giveaway when you play online and enter non-winning tickets.

Signature of Claimant _____

CT

DDP - Rev. 02/16   *Heat sensitive paper - Keep away from heat.*

Made in Michigan

MI-1002

290123251

PLEASE CHECK TICKET FOR CORRECT
DRAWING DATE(S), NUMBER(S) AND AMOUNT

RULES

THIS TICKET IS VALID ONLY FOR THE DRAWING DATE(S) PRINTED ON THE FRONT

All tickets, transactions and claims are subject to the laws of the State of Michigan, the rules, regulations, and all directives of the Michigan Lottery, and any changes thereto.

KEEP ALL WINNING TICKETS IN A SAFE PLACE. ALL PRIZES MUST BE CLAIMED WITHIN ONE YEAR OF DRAWING DATE. ANY CLAIM FOR A PRIZE MUST BE ACCOMPANIED BY AN AUTHENTIC WINNING TICKET WHICH IS CAPABLE OF BEING VALIDATED.

Winning tickets may be presented to an authorized Lottery retailer or any official Lottery office. Tickets which are illegible, altered, counterfeit, defective, unregistered, or which fail any part of the Lottery's validation tests are ineligible for prize payment.

Play Online at MichiganLottery.com for more chances to win cash instantly! Plus, earn Reward Points redeemable for entries in the Play It Again Giveaway when you play online and enter non-winning tickets.

Signature of Claimant _____

"I need to talk to Real," Constance said faintly as she took a seat at the custom all glass dining room table.

"You going to be ok, I got your back," B-low replied walking over and patting Constance on the shoulder.

Chapter 42

" *T*ake everything off and hand it to me one at a time." The fat white officer instructed as he kept a close eye on Real to make sure that he wasn't trying to conceal anything.

"Boxers too?" Real asked as a couple more inmates looked on waiting to be stripped next.

"You don't understand English boy, everything," the man spat as he searched every piece of clothing Real had on and then threw them on the floor.

Real was seconds away from punching the officer square in the face.

"Yeah, whatever," Real mumbled as he stood naked in the gym's bathroom floor.

"Bend over, squat and cough," the officer barked as sweat dripped from his forehead.

Real thought hard before he submitted to the officer's demand. He knew he had no win in his current position so he did what he was told. After the officer cleared him Real picked up his clothes, got dressed and exited the bathroom.

After being stripped, he and Tino found a spot on the crowded gym bench and patiently waited for the officers back down in the dorm to get finished searching their rooms.

"Man this shit too crazy, how long we suppose to be in this

hot ass gym?" Real asked Tino who watched the other inmates, begging the gym officer for a basketball so they could run a couple of games while they waited.

"Man ain't no telling. You good? That thang hid good ain't it?" Tino asked Real hoping Real had the shank pushed all the way to the back of the heater.

"Yeah it's straight."

Real and Tino sat around talking and watching the other inmates chase the basketball. They didn't notice the group of gang bangers huddling up on the far side of the gym floor. The OG of their set had just been passed a message, a half a million was being offered for Richard Walker aka Real's life. The OG called a meeting and discussed with his other bangers the best way to take care of Real.

"Look yall, I just got word that it's a half a million waiting on who ever took out a nigga name Richard Walker, do anybody know 'em?" Tuk asked his fellow gang members who stood around hungrily wanting a piece of the half million.

"Naw. Nope. Never heard of him," all the bangers chimed in.

"Look I'll get with lil Chubb that work in ID and find out who he is but until then yall get tooled up and ready to ride, ain't no way we going to pass up that half a mill," the OG said forcefully.

"Bro how you know the money good?" One of the bangers called out.

"The money is guaranteed. Just put it like this, the people high up getting a cut that nobody knows about but me…well us now," the OG said as he started dapping them up with their signature hand movement.

"Everybody return to the building!" The gym officer yelled, as he demanded the basketball from the men running up and down the gym floor.

"That's our cue," Tino said, as him and Real followed the crowd out of the gym door.

"Excuse me bro," Real said as he mistakenly bumped into the OG as they both exited the gym.

"No problem young blood," the OG replied as he headed up to I.D. to find out who Richard Walker was.

Real and Tino returned to the dorm hoping nothing was found in their room. Entering the dorm they noticed some room doors was closed and some was open. Looking closer Tino saw that his door was closed. After everyone had entered the seargent on the CERT team told everyone to lock down so now everyone who door was closed was still standing outside their door. The warden sat at the dorm control panel looking through the items found in the locked cells. After examining the items he gave the CERT team orders to lock the men who stood outside of their doors in the hole.

"Fuck!" Tino spat as the CERT officer handcuffed him and escorted him to the hole.

Real mouthed something to Tino as he passed his cell. Tino knew they had found his cell phone so he mentally prepared himself for the thirty plus days he would be in the hole. After they cleared the dorm everybody was free to come out of their room. Real cleaned up his property that was thrown everywhere and then headed downstairs to call Constance.

Chapter 43

" *What* the hell!" Real said as he pushed button after button on the prison's blue wall phone that wasn't working.

Real tried the other two wall phones and found out that they wasn't working either. Needing to talk to Constance bad, Real stepped over to Fly the dread from Miami room who he worked out with every now and then.

"Say Fly, bro I need a favor," Real said as he stepped in and pulled the door up behind him.

"What's up Real?" Dread asked getting up off the bed just in case Real came with trouble.

"Bro the phones down there ain't working and I'm trying to holla at my lady to see what's going on. Bro I need you to let me get a couple minutes so I can see what's going on," Real asked.

"Me boi Real, I don't have many minutes on me ting, if you can get a card you can use it," Dread replied sitting back down on the bed.

"I can swing that bro. I will get my girl to go get you one," Real assured him.

"Ok deal," Dread replied digging in his mattress for his phone.

Real got the phone from dread and rushed off to his room.

Telling his Mexican roommate he had to use the restroom Real closed the door and blocked the window. Real dialed Constance number and pressed send.

"Hello?" Constance answered not recognizing the number as she followed B-low out back to the guest house.

"Hey baby! What's going on?" Real asked excited to hear her voice.

"Baby damn—I've been waiting to hear from you! How you calling from a 404 number?" Constance asked confused and excited.

"I'm on my patna cell phone. What's been going on? Where you at?"

Real asked while peeping around the card board flap he had blocking the window looking for the officer.

"First I want to ask you about your trip to Miami. Why didn't you tell me?" Constance asked firmly not wanting to say too much on the phone.

"What trip?" Real asked, not sure what she was talking about.

"The Italians Real, I was attacked today in my office and…"

"That's Real," B-low called out as they entered the expensively furnished guest house.

"Who is that? What the hell going on?" Real asked getting heated.

"That's B-low I'm out at his place, he…"

"You out at his place! What the fuck going on?" Real snapped.

Constance could hear the anger in Real's voice.

"Ain't shit going on! Like I just said I was attacked in my office today!" Constance snapped back.

"Attacked! By who?" Real asked, calming down.

"Some lil Italian. B-low was stopping through and thank God he did because the man was waiting in my office." Constance explained.

"You ok?" Real asked knowing very well where the attack came from.

"Yeah, I'm alright but why they coming after me?" Constance asked faintly.

"They looking for revenge." Real said in a low tone thinking back on the day he killed Moretti and Rossi.

"What did you d…"

"This ain't the time, we will talk about it later. Put B-low on the phone," Real said firmly.

"What up bro? How's it going?" B-low asked Real as him and Constance walked through the guest house.

"What the fuck going on man? Why you tell Constance about Miami?" Real spat as he paced back and forth in his small cell.

"Man it's got to be the Italians! They out for some get back and just so happen today I was with Constance when she was attacked, but as you and I know they will be back. Bro, I told her because she refused to let me help her until I filled her in on what was going on," B-low explained as Constance looked at him with her arms folded over her chest.

"Look here, keep my lady safe bro. I don't care what it take and how much it cost, I don't want a hair on her head touched, feel me?" Real said firmly hating he couldn't be there to protect Constance himself.

"I got you. I told her to move into my guest house until everything calmed down. My word bro, she will be safe and secure at all times," B-low said as they walked through the guest house.

"Ok I'm counting on you. Put her back on," Real replied not really liking the fact that Constance was staying around another man, but he knew that was the only way she would be safe.

"Hello?"

"You going to be ok just roll with the program until I can get there. B-low is going to make sure you stay safe," Real said assuringly.

"Baby I ain't trying to be staying in no guest house. I'm not…"

"You going to stay in the guest house until I can put together a plan for you to get out of the state without anyone knowing. Just deal with the guest house for right now it won't be too long." Real insisted.

"Ok, but you need to come up with something fast because I ain't trying to be staying here," Constance declared as B-low stood watching her from the guest house bedroom doorway.

"I got you ba…"

"Knock! Knock!" The loud knock at the door startled Real.

"Yeah!" Real screamed standing close to the toilet just in case he had to flush the phone.

"CERT team coming across the field," The unfamiliar voice said outside of the door.

"Baby got to go police coming this way! Love you and as soon as I get my phone I will call you bye," Real said hastily hanging up the phone.

"Love you too! Bye," Constance said to a dead line.

" ome on baby let's take it in early tonight." Lace said seductively to Cash as she ran her tongue up and down his hard dick.

"Shit sound like a good idea, you go ahead on back while I lock up," Cash replied as he eased Lace head up from between his legs.

"Aight," Lace said faintly as she got up off the couch and headed back to the bedroom thinking of an excuse to double back so she could unlock the door for Black Bean.

Cash made sure Lace was in the bedroom while he hid the money. Before Cash headed back to the bedroom he grabbed the telephone cord off the front room phone and his 357 from the front closet. After thinking his plan through, he locked the front door and hid the gun in the small of his back. He peeped out the front window before he headed back to the bedroom.

"Damn boo, mama all hot and wet and you taking all day to cool me off," Lace cooed as she laid in the bed with nothing but her thong on.

"My bad baby I got you," Cash said as he came out his shirt making sure Lace didn't see the gun or the cord in his back pocket.

"Let me use the bathroom right fast you just get naked," Lace said softly as she rubbed her hands over his bare chest then hurried off to the bathroom in the hallway.

Cash knew that Lace was heading out to the front door to unlock it for whoever was on the phone. While she was gone he placed the 357 and the phone cord in the night stand draw.

"Where my hard dick at?" Lace called out as she reentered the room a few minutes later.

"Right here," Cash replied as he grabbed the front of his pants.

"Well come on and give it to me then," Lace said snatching her thongs off and laying back in the bed.

Cash walked over to the nightstand draw and pulled out the gun and cord as Lace laid spread eagle waiting for him to join her.

"What all that's for?" Lace asked puzzled.

"It's for you!" Cash said proudly as he reached over and grabbed a handful of Lace's hair.

"What the fuck you doing Cash! What's going…"

"Bitch you know damn well what's going on!" Cash screamed as he slapped her in the face with the barrel of the pistol.

"Cash please! Why you…"

"Whap!" The 357 connected again this time drawing blood.

Lace tried with all her might to get away from Cash grip but just couldn't get away.

After the third lick to the side of the face Lace stopped struggling and just laid out on the bed. Cash laid the 357 on the night stand then moved in and tied her hands behind her back.

"Cash why are you…"

"Bitch next time you try to set me up for a robbery make sure I don't hear about it," Cash spat as he reached over and grabbed her thongs and wrapped them tight around her head and mouth. When he got finished wrapping Lace up all she could do was lay there and look up at him. After securing Lace he positioned her in the middle of the bed and covered her up with the blanket.

Cash rushed through the apartment cutting off all the lights. While making sure everything was in place, Cash heard someone at the door. Knowing it was the person Lace was talking to earlier, Cash quickly grabbed the wood bat from the hall closet cursing himself for leaving the 357 in the bedroom laying on the night stand. Cash positioned himself just inside the kitchen doorway and waited for the person to enter the apartment and walk by.

Black Bean eased through the house like a cat stalking prey. Dressed in all black with a ski mask covering his face Black Bean crept quietly through the apartment with his 45 automatic out by his side. Peering down the long hallway to the brightly lit bedroom he saw someone moving under the covers on the bed. He smiled to himself—MY GIRL GOT THIS SUCKER WHIPPED—as he proceeded down the hallway in route to the bedroom. Just as he made his way through the dark front rooms and pass the kitchen the covers came off the person under the sheets.

"What the fuck!" Black Bean screamed as he zeroed in on Lace wiggling around in the bed like a fish out of water with her hands tied, a bloody face and thongs wrapped around her head.

Before he could react the bat connected with the back of his skull sending him crashing to the floor. Cash pounced on Black Bean with the bat striking him repeatedly until he was out cold. Satisfied with his work he grabbed Black Bean by the ankles and drug him into the bedroom where Lace stuggled to get free.

"Hey here's your folks," Cash said as he picked the limp intruder up and heaved him into the bed with Lace.

Lace looked on wild eyed at Black Bean all bloody and barely breathing. She knew if she didn't get loose she would surely be killed along with him. Reaching over Cash pulled the mask off the mans face.

"Black Bean! What the fuck you…" Cash started and the remembered Lace was from Black Bean part of the city.

Cash didn't know Black Bean personally. One night in the club his goon-B-low had pointed Black Bean out to him letting him know how notorious Black Bean was with his pistol play around the city. Cash would never forget the skillet black baldhead man with the long keloid gash down the side of his face. The same face Cash was looking at now all battered and bruised from the bat. Laying the bat down Cash walked over to the side of the bed and retrieved his 357 from the night stand draw.

"Um…um.mm," Lace squirmed wildly as Black Bean lay motionless beside her on the bed.

"No need to explain bitch you made your bed now lay in it," Cash spat as he pulled his shirt on and went to retrieve the bag of money and dope from the front of the apartment.

Lace pulled and pulled until the cord came loose. Just as she was about to totally free herself Cash came back in the room. Cash had the bag of money slung across his shoulder while holding a gas can.

"Yeah hoe you plotting with this nigga you die with this nigga! I hope the smoke don't get you before the flames," Cash said in a sinister tone as he started pouring gas around the room soaking the carpet and bed.

Spreading gas throughout the house, Cash grabbed a page out of the rap magazine that was laying on the table and made his way to the front door. Twisting the paper up, Cash pulled the lighter from his pocket and lit it. Throwing the flaming paper into the middle of the floor Cash slowly stepped out of the apartment into the darkness.

After Cash exited the apartment Lace hastily removed herself from the cord. Smelling the smoke and seeing the flames getting closer she frantically tried to wake Black Bean. Seeing it was no use she climbed out of her bedroom window into the night. When she looked back all she saw was orange flames shooting out of the apartment window. She said a silent prayer for Black Bean as she ran through the pitch black apartment complex plotting revenge.

Chapter 45

"Ɏ̸ou good?" B-low asked Constance after she got off the phone with Real.

"I ain't got no choice but to be," Constance said with disgust as she took in the lavishly decorated guest house.

"My guest house is fit for a queen. I know you use to bigger and better but this is it right now unless you want to stay in my room," B-low said jokingly, laughing out loud.

Constance rolled her eyes at him and walked off into the guest house bathroom. After inspecting her new living quarters Constance gave B-low a list of things she needed from her place. She felt uncomfortable sending him to get her underclothes and feminine products but he insisted that she stay inside where it's safe; at least until things calmed down.

"Could you please make sure your movers take it easy with my things and I know what I got I don't want none of my shit missing," Constance said forcefully.

"Calm down you ain't got to worry about none of that. My people are one hundred, they don't get down like that. You just make sure you write down everything I'm suppose to be getting," B-low responded with a hint of irritation in his voice.

Constance didn't respond she just handed B-low the slip of paper that she'd written her list on and walked off towards the guest house kitchen.

"Ain't no food in there!" B-low screamed as she walked off. "You welcome to hook something up in the main kitchen just make sure you make enough for two," B-low said as he exited the guest house in route to get Constance belongings and to close her office.

Just as B-low got half way through the house he turned and headed back to the guest house.

"Damn! Your keys and directions would help," B-low said sarcastically.

"You didn't ask and I still want the whole Miami story," Constance said firmly digging in her pocket for her keys and giving him her address.

"That's what the attitude all about? Look you going to have to holla at Real about that. All I can tell you is that it was a must that we handled the situation. Now we just got to be careful and cautious of all people and surroundings because you never know who is who. Just be cool and let everything die down until we can connect with the people behind this. My job is to keep you alive and I'm going to do it no matter how much attitude you give me," B-low told her as she handed him her keys.

"I'm cool, this is just…things just going too fast. It's not you, really…you saved my life today and I appreciate you but…I…I don't know," Constance said as she sat down on the arm of the soft money green leather couch.

"You ain't got to thank me, all I ask is that you just chill and work with me while I keep you safe. Just being straight up, if it wasn't for Real I wouldn't be sitting on a seven figure income. Bro really kept it real and gave me a chance in this shit. I gave him my word to keep you safe and that's what I'm going to do," B-low explained.

"I really do appreciate your help B-low. I won't ask you no more I'll just wait and speak with Real about Miami," Constance said humbly.

"Thanks. I'm going to make sure you are well taken care. I'm going to get all the stuff you need and make sure everything else is safe in storage," B-low assured Constance.

"Thanks," Constance said softly.

"If you really want to show your appreciation you could cook a nigga some real food. Eating all this fast food is going to clog my arteries!" B-low joked as he started for the door.

"I got you," Constance smiled.

"Deal," B-low smiled back as he exited the guest house, deep down lusting for the beautiful Constance.

Chapter 46

" *T*ake all flaps down, I need to be able to see in every
room! Take the paper out the back window too! Yall
see the CERT team coming this way damn!" Miss Johnson yelled
as she relieved the previous floor officer.

Miss Johnson was favored by all the inmates around the prison.
Miss Johnson was a hood rat in a uniform. She was also a mover
and shaker known to mule for the right price. She had befriended
Silk, a young player from Atlanta doing life; but after he put their
business in the street she cut ties with him. Miss Johnson wasn't
cute or fine she was just a down ass bitch which meant more to
the inmates at GSCP than a fat ass and cute face. Having been
around for years she knew how to play the game.

"Miss Johnson, where your clipboard at?" asked the CERT
team Seargent as he entered the dorm.

"Here you go," she replied as she handed him the clipboard
with the roster of all the inmates in her dorm listed in alphabetical
order.

"What was that name again?" The seargent asked the short
stocky CERT officer Green.

"Garcia," Green answered as he surveyed the dorm.

All the inmates was watching and hoping that the CERT team
weren't there for them. After finding the name on the clip board

they made way to inmate Garcia's room. The room in which him and Real shared.

Real watched them out of his cell window come up the steps and head in his direction. He hoped they would bypass his room. A few seconds later they were at his door. Real calmly dropped the cell phone in the toilet and flushed it as they opened his cell door.

"Get on the wall!" The CERT team officer yelled as the other two started searching the room.

Real got on the wall and stood still while he was pat searched. As he was being searched he looked out his door across the range at Garcia looking on intently as they ram shacked the room. After making sure Real was clean they told him to stand outside the door. Pulling everything out of Garcia's locker, the sergeant found a pack of bugler cigarettes filled with weed.

"Bingo!" The sergeant yelled as the other officers turned their attention to him.

"Let Wells out the hole, his information was correct. Round up Garcia and make sure his property is secure," The sergeant said as he exited the room with the bugler pack.

"Shit," Garcia mumbled to himself as he ducked off into his partner Pedilla's room to stash his phone.

"Everybody lock down!" The CERT officer Green yelled as he surveyed the dorm waiting on Garcia to come to the room. Real stood outside the door as the CERT officers started packing Garcia's property.

"Garcia?" The CERT officer Green asked as Garcia approached the room.

"Me speak no Engli," Garcia spat knowing he was on his way to lockdown.

"Yeah whatever. You understand these?" Green asked as he dangled his handcuffs in Garcia face. "Now turn around and put your hand behind your back," Green said with force as he slightly spun Garcia around and cuffed him.

Real looked on as they packed the rest of Garcia property and lead him out the dorm and to the hole. Before leaving they put Real in the room and locked the door. A few minutes later Miss Johnson started running the locks on the doors letting everybody back out. Before Real could step out the door good Dread was at his door.

"Me phone got to handle me business," Dread told Real as he looked around to make sure the coast was clear.

"Bro I had to flush the phone. What else was I suppose to do they would have found it anyway if I didn't." Real told him.

"No man, bad business! You pay me for phone," Dread said heatedly.

"Bro kill that tone I will get you another phone, but you ain't gonna make me do shit," Real fired back getting angry at Dread's aggression.

"No, no not like that, I just need another one, me low on money! Me can't afford to buy another," Dread explained thinking back on the other night when Real put the hands on Slim.

"I got you just hold tight, I'll have you one by tomorrow," Real assured him as Miss Johnson headed towards them making her rounds.

"Yall stay slipping around here," Miss Johnson said as she got up on Real and Dread.

Miss Johnson had her eye on Real since the first day she saw him. She hoped everyday in briefing that they would put her in the dorm with Real. She watched him discreetly as he worked out and mingled around the premises. She saw that he only fucked with a chosen few. She also saw that his right hand man Tino was in the hole. She was mesmerized by Real's exotic features and his well toned body. Being the boss bitch she referred to herself as she would keep her infractuation to herself.

"Shit happens," Real said looking at the thick, bad body hood rat up and down knowing she was digging him.

"Yeah it do," she replied returning Real's up and down

inspection.

"Me holla at you later," Dread told Real as he walked off after picking up on the discreet flirtatious dialog between the two.

"Yeah I got you," Real replied as Miss Johnson stood waiting for his attention to revert back to her.

"Where you from?" Miss Johnson asked, already knowing the answer.

"Atlanta," Real replied looking down at Miss Johnson's beat up finger nails and kool-aid stained uniform shirt.

"Oh you one of them Atlanta boys huh? How long you got?" Miss Johnson asked placing her foot up on the rail higher than needed trying her best to display her best assets, her funny shaped donkey ass and track runner thighs.

"A few more years, hopefully my lawyer can jump me before then. It's all good though, one way or the other," Real said as Miss Johnson sat staring at him.

"You married?"

"Naw, not yet. I'm engaged I got locked up before the wedding," Real replied, thinking about Constance.

"Dang, sorry to hear that but anyway do you got a phone?" Miss Johnson question caught Real totally off guard.

Real knew she was cool but he also was aware that she had on a correctional officer uniform sworn in by an oath. Real looked at her straight in the eyes and spoke.

"Why? You trying to get a nigga fucked up or something," Real spat.

"Nigga I ain't no fuckin police! I'm trying to give you my number," Miss Johnson fired back as she walked off to let the inmates coming from church in.

Real returned to his room and started cleaning up the mess the CERT team made and thought about Miss Johnson's interest.

Later that night B-low returned to the house with the items that were on Constance list. Having been out all day closing up Constance office, moving her stuff out her condo and putting it in storage, had B-low beat.

"This is what I'm talking about," B-low said looking down at the spaghetti and garlic cheese toast Constance cooked while he was gone.

"You need to do some grocery shopping—this is the last of your ground beef," Constance told him as she sat opposite him at the custom crafted cherry oak dining room table.

"I'll remember that. Is that all you need for now?" B-low asked as he watched the beautiful Constance move the fork in and out of her mouth as she ate the spaghetti.

"Yeah that's cool hopefully I won't have to be here too long," Constance said as she bit into the warm, crunchy garlic cheese toast.

"Yeah hopefully I can get to the bottom of this real soon," B-low said, not sure on the solution to solving the problem with the Italians.

While Constance ate dinner with B-low, across town Blanco called Angelo to update him on the day events.

"She had a fuckin monkey with her, fucker wouldn't go down,"

Blanco said angrily as he sat in his Blazer holding a bandage over his nose.

"I don't give a fuck if she had twenty monkeys get rid of her!" Angelo screamed into the phone.

"I will take care of her I just have to locate her again," Blanco assured Angelo as he mapped out his next move.

"She needs to be taken care of within twenty four hours no more excuses!" Angelo screamed and hung up the phone.

Blanco held the damp rag over his face as he navigated the blazer through the city to every location that Constance frequented. His search ended at her condo. Getting out of the blazer in the pitch black night and peeping in her window he saw that her place had been cleaned out. He knew now that locating her was going to be real difficult. Getting back in the truck he sped off into the night.

* * * * *

"Lock down! Lock down!" Mrs. Hall yelled over the dorm loud speaker as she flipped the switch to turn the dorm TV's off.

Before Miss Johnson left she made her way back up to Real's room and dropped off her number to him. Real accepted the number only because he knew she would be the perfect way to get what he needed.

"Say bro here you go," Old Man Stewart, the hole orderly said as he tossed Real a folded up piece of paper. "It's from Tino he said get at him."

Real opened up the letter as he stepped inside his room and closed the door. All inmates were to be locked in their rooms at 11:30 during the week and 1:00 on weekends. Real sat on his bed and read the letter…*Say bro, I need you to give old man Stewart some batteries and some smokes. I need you to holla at big boy and get that other thing for me too he know what I'm talking 'bout. Shit crazy bro, they caught a nigga slipping. Make sure you get at the old man with that and soon. I'm straight, I'll holla. One!*

"Lights out!" The officer yelled as she looked through Real's door window.

Real folded the letter back up cut off his light and laid back in his bunk. Thoughts of Constance consumed him as he drifted off into a light sleep.

he next day Real got with KP and picked up three phones one for him one for Dread and the one that Tino mentioned in the letter. After dropping Dread his phone off Real got with old man Stewart and dropped him Tino phone, two batteries, and some cigarettes. After making sure the coast was clear, Real headed up to his room to activate his phone unaware that around the prison the gangsters were looking for Richard Walker.

"Say patna you know a Richard Walker?" Scram asked Jay Bird, the medical orderly, hoping he had better luck than OG.

OG had went to I.D yesterday and his I.D connect wasn't working so now all his gangsters were out looking for Richard Walker aka Real. They were determined to find Real and take him out. The whole time Real never knew his life was in great danger.

"You talking 'bout Real, the rich nigga from Atlanta that owned that club G-Spot. Yeah that's BayBay—my roommate partner. He ain't been here too long. He the one that went hard on Slim and his boy. He in G building I think. I just hooked him up with a soft shoe profile last week. Why? What's up?" Jay Bird asked knowing Scram was nothing but trouble.

At the mention of BayBay name one of his gang rivals, Scram made sure that he kept his motives under wraps. Scram knew BayBay was a real killer. He also knew that when his friend Real was taken out it would be repercussions. He would consult with OG before he carried out his plan to go solo on Real and kill him.

"Ain't shit, my people said he was from my spot but they must be talking about somebody else cause you said he from the A," Scram explained. "I'll get at ya," Scram said as he walked off headed to the prison barber shop where OG and the rest of his gangsters congregated.

"Say Boss I just found out who Richard Walker is. He the one who rode on Slim Shady with that boy Tino," Scram told OG as their whole crew listened in.

"I know who you talking 'bout that's BayBay people," one of the bangers chimed in.

"Look here, we going to lay back and let Scram handle this nigga. We don't need a war between sets because right now we need to be getting our bread right. Scram catch him on the way from chow tonight he got to come round dead man curve. Make sure you serve him good we going to collect this money," OG said firmly as the other members listened in.

"I got ya I'm out," Scram said as he gave the crew the familiar hand movement and dashed off back to his dorm to get ready for tonight.

Real sat locked in his room with the flap up in the front window so no one could see in while he talked to the Verizon operator trying to activate his phone. Thirty minutes later he had a complimentary ten dollar credit and a working line. His first call was to Constance.

"Hello?" Constance answered as she sat in the guest house TV room going through some of her clients' files while looking at soaps.

"Hey baby. How you doing?" Real asked happy to hear her voice.

"Hey boo! You ok?" Constance asked excited to be talking to Real.

"I'm good baby. This is my new number I picked up my cell phone today. I need you to send old boy six hundred to this info," Real instructed

"Hold up let me get a pen."

"Hey boo, I'll just text it to you."

"Alright, six hundred? They cost that much?" Constance asked in amazement.

"Naw, I had to flush old boy piece when I talked to you the last time so I grabbed him another one too," Real told her as he paced his room talking on his new cell phone.

"Ok ill send it this evening. I'll be down there to see you this weekend too can't wait! I feel like I'm locked up too. I haven't left this house in over twenty four hours. B-low said he trying to fix the problem but I ain't risking it," Constance said laying the files to the side and laying back on the sofa enjoying her conversation with Real.

"I've been thinking. This is the move, you need to be looking for a spot out in California. I want you to relocate out there and lay low until I get home. I don't want no one to know where you are not even B-low. I want you to just disappear until I'm home," Real explained.

"Ok." Constance responded softly as she thought about Real's relocation demands.

She would not in any way dispute Real's instructions. She mapped out in her head how and when she would make her move. She knew it was going to take time to get in position. Right then she made plans to be out and in Cali in less than sixty days.

"Just let me know when you on your way. What's up with B-low? He been keeping you straight?" Real asked

"He's cool. He has helped a lot and if it wasn't for him I probably wouldn't be talking to you right now. Baby I'm scared I need you here with me," Constance broke down.

"Everything going to be ok I just want you to stay indoors and work on getting shit together for your move," Real said as he peeped out the flap on his door.

"I hear you boo. I can't wait for you to get home. I've handled all the business with the property the feds had and banked all the money," Constance informed Real

"Good we need a new start," Real replied.

"Yard call!" The old white dorm officer yelled letting the inmates know they were free and clear to go to the yard.

"Hey boo give me a minute I need to hit the yard to make sure my patna got his phone. Give me a minute ill hit you right back," Real told her then hid the phone in the heater with the shank.

Chapter 49

After leaving Lace and Black Bean for dead Cash headed out to the Broadway to check into a room for the night. The next morning he was awakened by his beeping cell phone.

"Say people this new flake just landed make sure you hit me when you jump what you got," Milkman told a half sleep Cash, still trying to take advantage of Cash with his high prices like he was green to the game.

Shaking the sleep off Cash replied thinking of his yesterday plans.

"Ok. What the tag is? I got my people coming through here from Atlanta headed to Miami to shop but if you can cut them some slack ill send them your way," Cash lied.

"Boy shit this here is that straight flake! I got to have at least twenty five a brick!" Milkman exclaimed.

"Boy, that's way too much, they buying too many to be hit in the head like that. I ain't even going to them like that. We'll just catch you on some more shit later," Cash said hoping Milkman would bite.

"How many they shopping for? If they buy more than six I'll fuck wit 'em on a better price," the greedy Milkman said.

"They trying to get bout ten but your price got to be right," Cash smiled as Milkman negotiated his own death.

"Aight, I'll do them for twenty two and that's the best I can do," Milkman said firmly agreeing to Cash's bogus deal.

"I know they will go for that. They should be in town in the next hour I'll call you when they get here," Cash told him while thinking of the best meeting spot to carry out his plans.

"Bet! Just hit me then," Milkman said excitedly while counting the profits he would make off of the ten fake dummy bricks of cocaine he was about to sell Cash and his patna's from the A.

* * * * *

"I can't believe this nigga!" Lace said to herself as she laid up alone in Larry—an old boyfriend's bed.

Last night after escaping out of the apartment window she ran to the nearest pay phone and called Larry her old boyfriend. She told him that her and her male friend had got in to it and he had beat her up and put her out. Larry being the nice guy that he was, not to mention still madly in love with Lace, got up out his bed and rushed down Poplar Street to pick Lace up.

Larry was too soft for Lace's taste; on top of that, he lived check to check. After a month together Lace called it off which Larry was totally against. Last night he was the only person that she could call to help her. He even gave her his bed while he slept on the sofa. When she woke this morning she saw that Larry had left for work.

"I swear this nigga going to pay for this shit! His snitching ass," Lace ranted and swore to herself as she gathered her thoughts.

After making a couple of calls to some old friends in Atlanta she laid back down until she heard the truck outside a couple hours later. The man pulled up in a white ford F-150 with dark tinted windows. Hearing the truck outside Lace bolted out the door and jumped in. The man in the truck wanted answers as Lace explained to him how the dude Cash which he knew of from around the way killed his brother Black Bean. Peanut wasted no time hitting his squad up on the westside of Atlanta and giving them the news. Lace knew that Peanut would waste no time finding and killing Cash.

* * * * *

Cash pulled up outside of Milkman apartment and blew the horn. Milkman stuck his head out of the door and waved Cash in. Cash got out with the black duffle bag that he had stuffed the hotel room phone books in. As he reached the door he heard voices inside. Hearing the voices made Cash reevaluate his plans.

Milkman had gave his young goons the plan. Seeing Cash pull up they all got ready to flim flam Cash and his Atlanta patna's with the fake dope. Milkman had instructed them to take the money from Cash and his people if he tried to back out of the deal. He hoped to make the lick easy but if it came to it they were ready to shed blood for the money.

"This nigga solo," Cash said to his lil young goons as he peeped out the curtains of the crackhead apartment that they used as their drug distribution spot.

"Sweet as cotton candy!" Quan,the oldest of the young click said, as he peeped out also watching Cash approach with the bag of money.

"Knock! Knock!"

"Yeah!" Milkman screamed from the chair he quickly retreated to as Cash got closer to the door.

"Cash," Cash called out as he adjusted his 9mm tucked in his waist.

"Come in!" Milkman screamed.

Cash walked into the dirty apartment with caution. All the men were sitting around smoking on weed and watching ESPN on an old TV.

"What it is people? What up with your folks from Atlanta?" Milkman asked, as he looked at Cash suspiciously.

"They back at my spot I got the money for their play," Cash replied surveying the room and each mans position.

Cash had made up his mind when he walked in to leave everybody dead and take all the dope and money they had. Seeing that it was three men, he positioned himself in front of the room in clear view of the men. He wanted to make sure he had a clean shot on all the men when he started shooting.

"Ok. How many you getting?" Milkman asked.

"Ten for now but if this shit can take some hits like you said we will be back no doubt," Cash said waiting on the right time to pull his gun.

"No problem. Like I said this shit is the truth! Hey Loco, grab me ten of them thangs from the back," Milkman called out to his lil do boy of the crew.

The bricks were taped, wrapped and had the stamp in the middle just like the real thing. Loco brought ten of the fake kilos from the back and set them on the table. Cash looked in amazement at the drugs. He knew he was about to be back on top again and this time he would be top dog and not a lieutenant.

"What that bread looking like?" Milkman asked Cash as he waited to be passed the bag of money.

The young goons looked on discreetly while set on ready if Cash tried to back out on the deal.

Cash knew it was now or never. As soon as he handed Milkman the bag he snatched his 9mm from his waist. His first couple of shots were aimed at the youngsters that sat on the sofa. Before the men could flinch Cash's bullets had immobilized both of them. Loco took one to the chest as Quan took two to the neck and head.

"Hey! Fuck! What up man!" Milkman screamed while holding the bag he had just got from Cash.

"Nigga you know what it is," Cash barked as he leveled the gun at Milkman.

"Bro please don't kill me! You can have it all! Shit ain't got to be like this! Please bro," Milkman pleaded as he dropped the bag.

"Nigga you must think I'm crazy! Now just for trying me, you get two instead of one!" Cash screamed as he sent two hollow tips through Milkman's skull.

Taking his time, Cash searched the house and got all the money and dope that was there. He even took the jewelry that the men wore. Satisfied with his take which was twenty thousand in cash and thirty bricks Cash made plans to set up shop and take over the city. What Cash didn't know was that the thirty dummy blocks were worthless.

" ino! Tino!" Real screamed into the front vent of building J-1, the hole.

Everyone was outside on the yard catching up on the prison gossip, smoking weed, drinking bom-bay's, and plotting the perfect murder.

"Look man hit 'em up in here," the OG said to Scram pointing at his own neck.

"I got you, this nigga is a done one," Scram said all geeked up ready for tonight.

* * * * *

"What's going on on the inside? Has Real been dealt with yet?" Angelo asked Michael.

"I spoke with my connect, he said he contacted the head of one of the deadliest gangs and they are working on eliminating him real soon," Michael explained

"Real soon! It needs to be done now! We're paying too much for real soon!" Angelo screamed into the phone.

"I will call back and press the issue. It shouldn't be…"
Angelo cut him off.

"Real needs to be dead by day break!" Angelo screamed and

hung up the phone.

Michael cleared the line and called his connect at the prison.

"GSCP may I help you?" The friendly voice on the other end asked.

"Yes, could you please connect me with chaplain Larson?" Michael asked as he thought about the man behind the cloak that was conspiring to commit murder.

A few seconds later he was on the line.

"Hi, may I help you?" the voice on the other end asked.

"Hey Kenneth what's going on?" Michael asked hoping the man had good news.

"Michael I can't talk to you right now! Didn't I tell you to never call me at work," Kenneth said through clenched teeth.

"It was urgent. Our plans need to be carried out today because my people are getting restless," Michael told him in a serious tone hoping he could speed up the process.

"I will look into it and call you back when I get off work. God bless," he spat and hurried off the prison phone line that was known to be monitored from time to time.

Michael hung up the phone and lit one of his most expensive cigars and smiled. He knew that after Real was killed he would be walking away with a half million dollars and his old friend Kenneth will be left holding the empty bag with gang members looking to be paid.

* * * * *

"Yeah!" Tino screamed from up under his door.

"You got that!" Real screamed back, trying hard to hear Tino from the back of the lockdown building.

"Yeah! Good looking out! I will get at you later," Tino screamed as he read the short note Real had sent with his new cell phone number on it.

"Check," Real said then started back across the yard to his building.

"Yo OG ain't that boy right there?" Scram asked as Real walked across the yard in their direction.

As Real continued in their direction he heard his name being called, it was Bay Bay with a crew of young bangers trailing.

"What it is bro? What the deal is?" Real asked as Bay Bay reached him.

"Say Real I need your help my nigga. I got this mule ready to look out for the right price but my ends fucked up. She will do whatever I just need the money to make shit move. My lil partner got a pound and four phones already sitting I just need the money to pop this shit off," Bay Bay explained.

"What's the tag bro? I got you," Real said without hesitation thinking about Bay Bay having to spend the rest of his life in prison.

"She wants a stack," Bay Bay replied, reluctantly hoping it wasn't asking too much of Real.

"Aight just let me know where to send it to," Real told him again without hesitation.

"Ok I'll just bring all the info out at chow call tonight. If they call yall out first just wait on me in the chow hall," Bay Bay told Real as he turned to walk off.

"Check that," Real replied as Scram and OG watched the exchange.

"He fuck with Bay Bay hard I see. Make sure when you go you go hard and don't leave this nigga breathing!" OG spat as Real walked by them to his dorm.

"Nigga good as dead no doubt," Scram fired back as they turned and walked back to their respective buildings.

Chapter 51

*B*efore leaving the house B-low went back to the guest house to check on Constance. Walking straight in, he startled her as she came out of the shower naked.

"Ah! What you doing!" Constance screamed trying to conceal herself as she rushed back in the bathroom for a towel.

"Damn my bad!" B-low screamed as he fixed his eyes on Constance perky C cups, thick thighs, and plump ass.

"You need to learn to fuckin knock," Constance spat as she stepped back out of the bathroom wrapped in a towel.

"Damn my bad," B-low replied smiling replaying the picture of a naked Constance back through his mind.

"Yeah whatever! What's up?" Constance asked angrily.

"I was just coming through to check up on you and to see if you needed anything," B-low said, giving Constance a thorough obvious look over as she stood in front of him in a pair of tight shorts and a tank top.

"I'm straight," Constance replied before heading to the back room and closing the door.

* * * * *

Blanco rode around the city for an hour and a half trying to locate Constance at all of her known locations. He knew Angelo was a very impatient man so he made it his business to stay out all day and night until he tracked Constance down.

* * * * *

"Aight I'll be back, just hit me on my cell if you need me," B-low said as he exited the guest house.

"Hey! B-low!" Constance yelled as she hurried out the back room to catch B-low.

"Yeah?" B-low replied hearing her calling him.

"I do need something. Could you go by my place and check my mailbox I had some very important paper work coming that I totally forgot about." Constance asked still mad at his intrusion.

"I can do that. I will swing by there after I handle my business. Anything else?" B-low asked as he undressed her with his eyes.

Every since he met Constance he had been attracted to her. Real had trusted him as a friend to look after her but his attraction was heavily outweighing the friendship he had with Real. Now that Real was going to be gone for some years and now that B-low was on top of the game he thought that he had a better shot at making Constance his. B-low had made up his mind to let it be known that he was feeling her tonight over dinner.

As B-low navigated the money green seven series BMW through the streets of Atlanta in route to Fair Street bottom he made a couple of calls to his Westside connects letting them know that he had seven bricks left for nineteen a piece. Before he hung up the phone all seven was sold. Dropping the dope off at his runners apartment and giving him the connects number and specific instructions on what to do with the money he headed off to Constance condo.

Pulling up at Constance condo he got out and checked the mail box. He grabbed a small brown package and a couple of home security flyers out the box and then got back in the car. The Blazer followed as he pulled off in route back to the house. It didn't take Blanco long to recognize the man that he fought with not long ago. Blanco thanked God for his luck. He smiled as he followed B-low, he was more than happy now that he could finish his job.

Pulling up at home, B-low grabbed Constance's mail and headed in the house not noticing the Blazer that followed at a discreet length behind him.

B-low got out the car and headed straight back to the guest house. He knocked on the door.

"Come in," Constance yelled from the couch where she sat looking at the finalized sales paperwork on her and Real's mansion.

"Here you go," B-low said as he walked over to her on the couch and gave her her mail.

"Thanks" she replied not looking up.

"No dinner? I go way to the other side of town to get your mail and you ain't even hook a nigga up a plate. That's fucked up," B-low said jokingly.

"You ain't say nothin 'bout no dinner and I ain't your bitch. You need to get you some live in pussy nigga. This my last time cooking you dinner." Constance said playfully as she opened up the mail.

"My last meal. Yes ma'am," B-low uttered, smiled and walked off.

The whole time B-low and Constance debated over dinner Blanco sat outside a few feet from the house in his blazer trying to figure out the best way to get into the mansion. He planned to make his move around midnight when he figured they would be sleep. Constance went to the main house and started dinner while B-low retired to the den with a bottle of Hennessey and a couple of ecstasy pills. Blanco sat devising a plan while B-low was finishing off his third glass of Hennesy while he waited for dinner.

"Food's ready," Constance called out thirty minutes later while sitting their plates of fried fish and french fries on the table.

"That's what I'm talking about," B-low said as he stepped into the room, sat down at the table more than tipsy from the Hennesy.

"Last meal," Constance said playfully as she sat in front of him.

The whole time they ate B-low stared at Constance. Not noticing his drunkin stares Constance finished eating and told B-low she would handle the dishes tomorrow because she had to get back to the guest house so she wouldn't miss Real's call.

Out of nowhere B-low snapped.

"Fuck Real!" B-low said with aggression catching Constance totally off guard.

"Excuse me! What the fuck did you say?" Constance fired back making sure she heard him right.

"You know you want to fuck with a nigga! Quit playing and get with this shit," B-low spat as the alcohol and pills took over.

"Nigga you fucking crazy! Real made your ass now you sitting here disrespecting him! I'm getting up out your shit first thing in the morning!" Constance screamed not believing what she was hearing.

"Fuck that shit come here," B-low said forcefully as he reached over and grabbed her from across the table.

"Nigga get the fuck off of me," Constance said as she tried to pull away.

"Come here!" B-low screamed as he pulled her to him and started kissing her on the face and neck.

"No, get off me!" Constance screamed lifting her knee, connecting with his most private part.

"Bitch!" B-low doubled over as he screamed out in pain.

Constance bolted to the guest house to get her phone and keys. She hurried out to her car but before she could climb behind the wheel B-low was grabbing her trying to pull her clothes off. Breaking free from B-low she bolted from the garage out into the dim lit streets straight into Blanco's path.

Chapter 52

" C how call! Chow call!; Last call for chow!" screamed the old white male dorm officer that was filling in for Miss Johnson.

All the men crowded the door filing out for the slop in the chow hall that they referred to as food. Real was just about the last one out, delayed because he had to stash his phone in the heater before leaving.

"Hold up, tuck your shirt in," the old man ordered stepping in front of Real.

Real took a deep breath and then forcefully jammed his shirt in his pants. Not in a rush being that the line was out the chow hall door, Real looked around for Bay Bay. The yard was packed with inmates coming and going to chow, going to pill call and just out walking around being that it was almost dark out and yard call most definitely would be cancelled for tonight.

"There he go right there!" The old gang banger Anthony Strickland aka Third Born screamed to Scram that was walking slightly ahead of him.

"Where?" Scram asked looking around the yard.

"About to go in the chow hall," his banger partner Third Born said pointing in Real's direction.

"Aight I got this nigga just get Sed so yall can block the scene while I get at this nigga."

"Ok. We will be on the corner by the mailbox when he come out," Third Born said and quickly made a detour to go and get the other banger.

Scram eased up in the chow hall and stood in line directly behind Real. He sized Real up and knew from his bulging muscles that he had to go hard when the time was right. Real never looked back while he waited in line for his tray.

"Yo Real!" Bay Bay screamed from across the chow hall with his hand in the air.

Real, looking up, gave him a head nod letting him know that he saw him then headed over to the table where BayBay sat with two of his goons.

"What up bro? Here go that info, I appreciate you handling that for me," Bay Bay told Real as the two goons got up to leave.

"We out, Bay." The 6'4", deadly big man that was only twenty-one years of age told BayBay as him and another oversized young banger stood to leave.

"I will catch yall later," Bay Bay replied as he sat waiting on Real to finish the gravy covered meat pattie and potatoes.

Scram sat watching Real and Bay Bay, glad that the other two men had left. Now all he needed was for Bay Bay to leave. Scram knew his bangers would take care of Bay Bay if needed but this move was only for Real and besides they didn't want it to turn into a gang war because right now they were on some get money shit.

Real and Bay Bay got up put their trays in the window and exited the chow hall into the night darkness with Scram close behind. Scram looked ahead of the men and saw his two bangers at the mailbox waiting for his move. Scram knew the hit had to go down tonight. He would have to let his bangers take care of Bay Bay if he interfered.

As Scram neared the mailbox he gripped the sharp pointed steel rod tight causing the veins to pop out his hand. As Real and

Bay Bay neared the mailbox where Third Born and the other banger waited Scram moved in like a cat hunting prey. Just as Scram was rearing back with the shank Real glanced back and saw him.

"Hey! What in th…" Real started as he weaved out the way.

Real weaved Scram coming down with the shank but when he moved to the side it left the whole side of Bay Bay neck and face open, the steel rod penetrated Bay Bay's neck with ease he never saw it coming. Scram, pulling the shank back for another attack was met with a fist in the side of the head by Real. Scram stumbled as the force of Real blow knocked him off balance.

Bay Bay laid lifeless in a puddle of blood with a gaping hole in the side of his neck. Real seeing his friend laid out in his blood moved in on Scram not caring about the shank he held. Just as Real moved in he was attacked from behind. Third Born discreetly stepped into the malay. The steel rod penetrated Real's side, stopping him instantly. Scram seeing Real stunned pounced on him quickly, sticking him repeatedly as Real fought back wildly trying to get away from the men.

After seeing that Scram had Real under control Third Born and the banger slyly eased off while Scram resumed his attack on Real. Scram cursed out loud at Real's resilience. Real would not go down. Just as Scram positioned himself for his death blow a man screamed out from behind.

"Hey you! Drop that!" The young freckle face rookie officer that was clearing the walk yelled.

Real was staggering trying his best to stay on his feet. Scram saw the officer running to the scene so he took off, shank in hand. It was Scram lucky day, as he neared his dorm the door was wide open while the dorm officer was standing to the side smoking a black and mild. Scram eased in the dorm unnoticed by the smoking guard and headed straight to his room and cleaned himself up.

"10! 10!" The rookie yelled in his radio as he surveyed the

bloody scene.

Real couldn't stand any longer. After a couple minutes he passed out on the sidewalk in his blood soaked clothes. Officers from all over rushed the scene. Seeing all the blood they radioed for the medical cart. When the medics arrived they knew from all the blood that the men had to be rushed to the hospital.

The EMT's rushed the scene fifteen minutes later. Bay Bay was declared dead and Real was rushed to the hospital barely living. All the dorm windows was full of inmates looking on as the medics removed the men. Before the night was out rumors around the prison was that Real and Bay Bay were dead, killed by a crazy Mexican.

OG smiled as he looked out at the scene. He counted the half a million over and over in his head. Scram took a shower fixed him a Bombay and sat down in front of the TV like nothing had happened. Deep down he prayed that the prison officials never found out he was behind the bloody men on the sidewalk. Real gasp for air as they wheeled him to the emergency room.

onstance couldn't believe B-low had attacked her. As she walked down the dark street she pulled out her BlackBerry and looked up the number for a taxi cab service. After calling a cab she dialed Real's number.

"The party you have reached is not available please leave…" When the beep sounded Constance started leaving a message.

"Real this nigga B-low tried to force himself on me baby! I'm so tired of this shit please call me! I left, I'm walking down his street now waiting on a cab. I'm scared baby! I started to call the police but I know that was out of the question. I need to talk to you baby! I want you home! I'm just going…"

Constance stopped in her tracks after hearing someone behind her.

"You got away once but you won't get away this time," a voice called out from behind Constance.

Constance turned and looked into the face of the man that tried to kill her in her office.

"Who are you! Please leave me…Ah! No!…Ah! Please! Ah!" Blanco moved in quickly and grabbed her. He pulled his hunting knife from his pants cargo pocket and repeatedly stabbed Constance.

Constance dropped her cell phone and tried her best to get

away from Blanco but he held on to her tight. He reared back time and time again with the hunting knife, slashing Constance. Constance begged and pleaded for him to stop as the blood started to soak her clothes. After being stabbed over twenty times she gave in and fell to the ground. Blanco stood over her grabbed her by her hair and pulled her head up. With one swift stroke he slit her neck and released her hair. Her limp body fell to the ground with a thump. Real's voicemail recorded Constance, the love of his life being murdered.

* * * * *

B-low went back in the house and slammed the door after Constance bolted from the garage. Still tipsy from the alcohol he went up to his bedroom and fell face first into his king size custom designed bed. He was awakened a few hours later by a loud knock on the front door. He pulled himself from the comfortable bed and took the long walk to the front door.

"Who is it?" B-low asked still a little high off the pills and alcohol.

"Police, could we speak to you for a minute," the two uniformed, hulking white officers asked, standing outside his door with pen and pad in hand.

B-low wondered what this police visit was about. He didn't keep dope in his spot so he wasn't worried about them trying to catch him down bad. Then he thought about Constance and cursed to himself, he knew this had to be about her. Thinking that she had called the police on him he concocted a quick story and opened the door.

"Hi may I help you?" B-low asked sleepily.

"Sorry to wake you sir but we are canvassing the area to see if anyone recognizes this woman," the young muscle bound officer asked holding out Constance drivers license that they got from her purse that was laying next to her dead body.

"No, I don't recognize her," B-low lied looking at the license picture sideways as the officer held it out."What's going on? Should I lock myself in the house?" B-low asked jokingly as he looked up the road at all the flashing blue lights and the crowd of people lining the street.

"She was found dead out in the road someone stabbed and cut her up real good. It don't make no fucking sense how they did her," The officer said with disgust.

"What! **DEAD?**" B-low screamed then regained his composure. "Someone killed the girl on the license? That's messed up," B-low said surprisingly, as he thought about last night.

"Yeah someone out here have no regards for human life. If you hear anything could you please contact us," the officer said as he handed B-low his official card with his number on it.

"Will do." B-low said as he closed the door and took a deep breath.

"Fuck!" B-low cursed out loud as he walked out to the guest house where he planned to get rid of all signs of Constance.

B-low knew he had to contact Real and give him the news. He promised Real that he would keep Constance safe and he had let him down. He knew it had to be the man from the office. The man knew where he stayed. As he picked up around the guest house sleepiness had took over. B-low sat on the couch and a few minutes later he was fast asleep.

Chapter 54

*L*ater that night Cash sat in his hotel room and counted his take. He stacked the bricks of cocaine on the hotel room counter and made a couple of calls.

"Yeah?" Turk answered wide awake with people screaming and cheering in the background.

"Say my guy, I know it's late but I wanted to let you be the first to know that I just got a shipment in and everything's going for the low low," Cash explained as he looked over at the bricks neatly stacked on the counter.

"What you talking bro?" Turk asked as he retreated to the backroom of his sports bar to get away from the noise.

"You get more than three I will give 'em to you for eighteen a piece straight up and down," Cash told Turk as he pointed the remote at the TV and started flipping channels.

"Eighteen a piece? What if I snatch ten?" Turk asked as he stood in the sports bar back room that he used as an office.

"The best I can do for ten or more is seventeen five," Cash said as he stopped the TV on BET.

"Aight. I will call you tomorrow and I'm looking to grab ten but if my lieutenant don't make a drop by the morning I'll just get seven."

"That'll work just holla when you ready," Cash told Turk and ended the call.

Cash smiled as he stared at the bricks he took from Milk Man and his crew. He ran the figures through his head. He added what he had with the take and started tingling all over. He knew he was well within the million dollar range. While watching Lil Wayne and Bird Man rep New Orleans Cash propped up on a pillow and fired up a blunt.

* * * * *

The next day OG hurried off to the chaplain office.

"Everything is taken care of—you can have the money delivered here." OG handed Kenneth a piece of paper with an address on it as he walked into the prison Chaplain's office.

"He's not dead yet. He is in critical condition right now we have to wait for the outcome before any money is exchanged," Kenneth told OG as he peeped out of his office blinds at the prison warden and top brass getting ready for inspection.

"He's not dead?" OG asked confused.

"No. The other guy is the one that was killed. I came to you to handle this job but you seem to keep falling short. Maybe I need to go speak with Piru about taking care of this Richard fella," Kenneth said calmly referring to OG's gang rival with his back to OG still looking out the window.

In a swift motion OG wrapped his arm around the chaplain neck and positioned a shank to the side of his face.

"Look here you coward bitch you ever disrespect my gangster again I will leave you stankin' up in this bitch! The job will get done and when it does, you better have every penny of the money. Now find out what's up with Real and let me know when he arriving back on compound," OG spat, pushed the chaplain face first into the wall and slammed the door as he walked out of the office.

* * * * *

The stabbings were the talk of the compound. It didn't take Tino long to get the news. Even though he hadn't known Real that long he still had love for him like a brother. Tino contacted some of his connects to find out who was behind the hit. Before the day was out he knew about the money being offered, the gang behind it and the man that stabbed Real.

Tino called one of his lil mission men that he left back in the dorm and told him to go to Real's room and get his phone from the heater and send it over to him in the hole. After making sure all Real belongings were secure he called his partner in crime and one of the prisons most feared men Yaki.

Yaki was down for triple murder with life without parole. He was an animal without a conscience. Yaki and Tino were good friends. Yaki was known to go hard with his tool whenever he had a problem. Tino explained what happened to Yaki and they planned to take care of Scram and everybody else involved. Tino had twenty eight days until he got out the hole, a blood bath was in the near future.

The hole orderly delivered Real's phone to Tino later that night. Taking it out of the Bugler pack Real had it wrapped in, Tino saw that Real had left it on. Real had over ten missed calls where someone had left voicemails. Seeing that it was set on lock Tino turned it back off and placed it back in the cigarette pack and stuffed it in his mattress. Just as Tino turned the phone off detective Long that was investigating Constance murder was dialing the number for the fourth time trying to see who Constance was talking to just before she was murdered.

Chapter 55

The next morning B-low woke up in the guest house with a splitting head ache and a hangover. He shook off his sleep and thought back on last night events.

"Fuck," he cursed out loud faulting himself for Constance murder.

Getting up and getting rid of all of Constance belongings he got in her car and drove it out to the airport and left it. After making sure the car had no signs of him anywhere he flagged down a cab that had just dropped off a couple looking like they were going on vacation. Riding in the back of the cab on the way home all he could think about was Constance. Arriving back at the house twenty minutes later he tipped the cab driver twenty dollars, jumped out the cab and rushed back in the house.

* * * * *

Real had been upgraded to stable condition and moved into a regular room. His lungs had been punctured and he was lucky to be alive because the shank came inches away from his heart. Real was guarded by two correctional officers as he laid in the hospital bed. Looking at all the bed controls he pressed the button to lift the head of the bed up, grabbed the remote and turned the

TV on.

"Somebody feeling better I see," The slim, petite female officer said, as Real flipped channels on the TV.

"Yeah I'm cool," Real said, as he put the TV on the news.

"Good, so now we won't have to keep working overtime making sure you don't escape," her male counterpart spat with a frown.

"Yeah, whatever," Real spat back as he put the TV on the channel 2 news.

The two officers sat, flanking the bed as Real watched the news and thought about revenge. He hoped that Bay Bay was ok. No one had informed him that Bay Bay was dead.

Real turned up the TV when the female reporter came on the screen with a late breaking news story...

This just in, the well known and highly respected realtor to some of Atlanta's richest and most recognized figures has been murdered. Constance Alexander was found dead in the middle of the street in the Highland Hills neighborhood that's known for its million dollar homes and sixteen hole golf course. A resident coming home from a late dinner date spotted her laying in middle of the street. When police got to the scene they saw that she had been stabbed repeatedly and her neck had been slit. No motive or suspect has been named in the case. We will keep you updated as information becomes available...

Real was speechless and in shock. He stared at the TV in total disbelief. He dropped the remote and closed his eyes. A single tear ran down the side of his face as his whole body went numb. The two officers paid him no attention as he silently screamed for his baby, his best friend, his soon to be wife.

* * * * *

B-low hated to have to give Real the bad news after he promised

Real that he would keep Constance safe. He had no way of getting in contact with Real but he knew in due time Real would get in contact with him to find out why he hadn't heard from Constance.

Putting the Constance situation in the back of his mind B-low pulled his cell phone from his pocket and called Juan at his clothing store that was located in the affluent area of Jacksonville.

"Hey Juan I need to grab ten outfits do you have a size ten in stock?" B-low asked talking in codes.

"Yeah my friend just come on down to the store and I will take care of you," Juan said as he did a quick count in his head of the kilos he had stashed in his warehouse.

"Do you have them in stock or am I going to have to wait for them to be delivered?" B-low asked hoping that they were on hand.

"We have them in stock just come on down," Juan said, assuringly.

"Ok. I am on my way," B-low told him as they ended the call thinking about the seven hour drive to Florida.

B-low had been doing big numbers in the dope game since Real was gone. He knew he owed all his fame and fortune to Real. He hated he had let him down with Constance. B-low went down to his office opened the safe and grabbed eight stacks of the neatly wrapped money. A few minutes later he was on his way out to Juan's store in Jacksonville. He promised himself this was his last time riding dirty, he would find him a mule as soon as he returned to the city.

Chapter 56

" *M*an this shit here is that straight flake! Fish scales bro,"
Cash told Turk as they stood in the empty sports bar
looking over the twelve kilo's of fake cocaine stacked up on the
tournament size pool table.

"You said you had me a good tag on 'em, what we talking?"
Turk asked thinking about the profits he was about to make off
the bricks.

"For you since you since this is your first time shopping
with a nigga give me sixteen a brick. I know you can't beat that
nowhere," Cash said with assurance.

"I can't complain, give me a minute," Turk said as he headed
back to his office to get the money.

Thoughts of just taking Turk for the whole bag crossed Cash's
mind but he quickly dismissed the thought. It was time to lay the
pistol down and get back into the streets with his work.

A few minutes later Turk returned with a bag of money.

"Here you go all to the penny," Turk told Cash as he handed
Cash the money and grabbed the bricks off the pool table and
placed them one by one in his office closet.

They both wasn't worried about counting the money or testing
the dope. They both knew each other's reputation so they knew
bad business was a death sentence.

After making the sale Cash jumped in the car with the bag of money and headed back out to his hotel room. It felt good to Cash to be officially back in the game. He pulled up into the hotel parking lot, grabbed the bag and headed in.

"Damn I love the game," Cash said calmly to himself as he pulled a neatly rolled blunt from his pocket and laid back on the bed.

He still didn't realize that he had just sold Turk, a straight up killer twelve bricks of fake cocaine.

* * * * *

"This is that straight flake! Fish scale," Turk told Junebug-one of Macon's biggest dealers and most treacherous man, mimicking Cash's words.

They sat in Junebug's car customization shop discussing a fair price for five bricks.

"Fuck with me on this five and I will come back with extra on the next play," Junebug demanded more than asked trying to intimidate young Turk.

"Nah bro, you get what your money can buy. I'm already giving you a killer price," Turk replied not one bit scared of the man that sat in front of him with the bad reputation.

Junebug leaned back in the hard steel chair and smiled.

"Aight lil nigga give me three," Junebug said impressed with Turk's firm stand.

"Money first," Turk said as he got up to get the bricks.

Junebug smiled.

"Give me a minute," Junebug said as he walked to his back office and then returned a few minutes later with the money.

Turk and Junebug went through this same thing every time they meet for a sale. Turk never gave in and Junebug always tried to intimidate Turk.

"Good deal," Turk said reaching for the bag of money.

"Slow your roll," Junebug said pulling the bag of money back.

Where's the product."

"Coming right up," Turk said as he went out to his truck and retrieved three kilo's from the bag that contained several kilos.

"Red tape?" Junebug said looking over at the bricks that were not wrapped like his usual buy.

"Yeah, new product."

"Cut it open," Junebug demanded looking at the unfamiliar wrappings.

"No problem," Turk said as he used the pocket knife that was attached to his key chain to split the red tape that concealed the cocaine.

After Turk cut the kilo open, Junebug walked over to inspect it closer. Looking at the texture of the package made Junebug double take. Then the aroma it gave off was not a cocaine smell, it smelled like biscuits. The package contained flour and a unfamiliar substance. Seeing the fake dope Junebug swung without warning hitting Turk in the face. The blow took Turk totally by surprise but he saw the same thing Junebug saw, a fake kilo.

Turk stumbled backwards, reached in his waist and pulled out his glock. As Junebug charged him, he let off two shots hitting Junebug in the chest. Seeing Junebug go down, he hurried to remove all traces of himself from the shop. On the way out the door he looked back at Junebug lifeless body and cursed out loud.

"Bitch nigga you mine!"

All the way back out to his spot all Turk thought about was murdering Cash.

Chapter 57

The doctors had cleared Real to leave and he was immediately transported back to GSCP by the two officers in a white DOC van. Arriving back at the prison Real was taken to ID so he could be reassigned housing and issued linen and his property.

"Damn son you fucked with the wrong nigga," The baldhead, fat, black ID officer joked looking at Real's bandages.

"Naw the wrong nigga done fucked with me," Real spat as he the officer walked to the back to get Real's property.

"Aight here you go. Get you a mattress and pillow from the first holding tank," the officer instructed as Real loaded his property onto the cart on wheels.

"What building I'm going to?" Real asked.

"It's your lucky day, you going back to your same room," the officer replied as he handed Real a combination lock and I D.

Real rolled the cart out of the I D room and out onto the compound. As he headed to his building he looked around for the man that attacked him. As Real went through the gate he looked over at the spot that still had signs of his and Bay Bay's blood splatter, he instantly became enraged.

On the ride back from the hospital is when he found out his friend's fate. Bay Bay was dead. As Real rolled the cart down the walk thinking about Constance and Bay Bay he transformed

into a mad man with nothing to lose. Real couldn't believe that
his baby girl was gone. His eyes watered as he descended the
sidewalk. As he reached the hole building he heard someone
calling his name.

"Real! Real," Tino called out from the backyard where he was
caged in.

Real was snapped out of his trance when he heard his name
being called.

"Yeah bro!" Real yelled through the crack in the cement wall
that separated them.

"You aight? I got the word on everything! I know it's going to
be hard but just lay low bro. I just found out they fucked up my
D.R. I will be out tomorrow we going to see bout them bitch ass
niggas!" Tino screamed as he paced around the cage like a savage
beast.

"Real talk bro! Bay Bay's gone my nigga," Real said in a sad
tone.

"What? They killed your lil homie! Bro just go lay low til
tomorrow. I'm going to send your business by the orderly. I will get
at you tomorrow," Tino yelled surprised at the news of Bay Bay's
death.

He had heard Bay Bay was killed the night it happened. He
was even told Real was dead too but he knew rumors floated
around prison like they floated around a beauty salon, nigga's was
worse than bitches with the rumors.

"Aight," Real said, as he continued on to his dorm.

As he passed the buildings on the way to his building inmates
was pointing and talking. Just as he rounded the corner he saw the
old gang banger they referred to as OG.

"What up player?" OG asked as Real pushed the cart on by
him and Third Born whom Real did not recognize from the night
of the assault.

"What up?" Real replied, as he walked on by still looking
around for the man that attacked him.

Reaching his building he guided the cart with his belongings through the door and positioned it at the bottom of the steps and unloaded his property. A few guys came over and helped him take his stuff to his room.

Chapter 58

The most expensive clothes hung from the racks of Juan's exclusive clothing store that was located in the wealthiest part of Jacksonville, Florida. Juan made a few calls right after getting off the phone with B-low. Juan had the whole south on lock, if you was moving any kind of drug more than likely it came from Juan.

The federal agent posing as a customer took pictures of Juan, his store, and a few customers. Juan had been under federal investigation for years now. The feds had been trying to pin his father Pablo for some time now but they could never get a guilty verdict on the old man. They knew his son wouldn't be so clever. The new generation was not as careful as the old. They tapped in on Juan's cell phone on numerous occasions and also took pictures of him out partying with his buyers. The feds loved how sloppy the new generation played the game, it made their job real easy.

* * * * *

After getting all his property to his room, Real made up his bed and laid down for a minute to think. He was glad the room was still empty so he wouldn't have to be bothered with a roommate trying to talk and kick it. He pulled the door closed and pulled out his photo album that contained his and Constance's pictures. As he laid on the bed and flipped through the pictures his heart got heavy. Tears flowed down his face as he stared at his baby Constance smiling and hugging him outside of the house. Real had not shed a tear since childhood but now he couldn't stop them. He promised Constance someone would pay for her murder.

Hours later there was a knock at Real's door.

"Yeah!" Real screamed angrily as he laid on his bunk in total darkness.

"The nigga that work the hole told me to get this to you, it's from Tino," the familiar voice said outside the door, as a potato chip bag wrapped up tight was slid under Real's door.

"Appreciate that Dread," Real replied as he grabbed the bag off the floor that contained his cell phone and a note from Tino.

Real wasted no time clicking on his light and reading the note.

Say bro, make sure you hit me and let me know you got your flop and this kite. Man I know who got at you and why. Them bangers was offered big money to off you bro and I ain't talking 'bout no couple stacks. A half million bro straight up and this comes from a reliable source that's affiliated with the bangers. They sent they lil mission man Scram at you, the other two nigga's was Third Born and Kyle. I hit my patna on the other side and he ready to ride on these bitches as soon as I get out the hole which should be tomorrow. Bro get tooled up and ready to ride, it's time to teach these niggas a lesson the A-town way! Yeah and the old nigga OG is the head man, yeah we got to see him too. Get at me though I'll holla.

Real was surprised at the news of the hit. He knew that kind of money had to be from the cartel. The same men that just had his baby Constance killed. Real wasn't going to waste any time trying to figure it out he had made up his mind to just fuck up everyone of the niggas that looked to collect for his life. OG was at the top of the list.

He unwrapped his cell phone and pushed the power button. As the phone came on the message icon popped up letting him know he had several unheard messages. He knew before he listened to them that they were all from Constance. The first one was just her telling him to call her and that she loved him. Hearing her voice made his heart heavy. He clicked the light off and laid back on the bed. After listening to the first message he pressed four to skip to the next. Real was stunned as he listened in closely to the next message...

Real! this nigga B-low tried to force himself on me baby! I'm so tired of this shit please call me! I left I'm walking down his street now waiting on a cab. I'm scared baby! I started to call the police but I know that was out of the question. I need to talk to you baby! I want you home! I'm just going...Who are you! Please leave me...Ah! No!...Ah! Please! Ah!...

Real heart sank as he listened to the man kill his baby girl. His eyes watered as his grip on the phone tightened. He couldn't control his tears as he laid in the bed he let out a loud scream that woke up most of the men in the dorm. He slammed the cell phone against the wall causing it to shatter in to pieces and slammed his fist into the thin mattress over and over again. Real promised death to the Italians responsible for Constance murder and planned to make B-low pay with his life as well. Real was not the same man he was when he came in, he was now about to show muthafuckers his true self, starting with the niggas tomorrow on the yard!

Chapter 59

B-low hated to make the trip to Florida but it was a must. He hated to have to ride dirty all the way back to the A but he knew that sometimes you had to get down and dirty and go against the grain for the fast money. Seeing the constant traffic he knew he would not make it before night fall. He picked up his phone and dialed Juan number.

"Yeah," Juan answered knowing it was B-low.

"Traffic crazy I'm going to be running late. I will call you from my hotel room tomorrow and let you know when I'm on the way," B-low explained.

"Ah man I had reserved you a spot at one of my good friend's party tonight! A lot of pretty women are going to be keeping us company all night," Juan said with emphasis.

"I hate to miss out just give me the ups on the next one," B-low said sticking by his rules, never mix business with pleasure.

"Ok B just call me tomorrow when you are on your way," Juan said as they ended the call.

As B-low rode down the highway he thought back on the day Real agreed to put him on. He so much regretted his actions of the night of Constance's death. He swore off the pills and alcohol for good for the effect they had on him. Riding through South Georgia he came up with a plan. He was going to grab a couple more million out the game, start him a construction company and lay back. The stress of the game had really taken a toll on him.

* * * * *

Cash laid up in the hotel room high and horny. He thought about Lace for a minute then pictured her dead, all burnt up in the apartment bed with Black Bean. Quickly dismissing the thought he picked up the phone and called this white stripper named Pinky that was built like a sister with hips and ass for days that he had met the other night at the club.

"What's up Miss Lady?" Cash said as she answered the phone looking to get Pinky to his room for the night.

"What's up? Who this?" Pinky asked as she pushed her Beamer down the highway in route to the cush trap.

"This Cash, from the club the other night," Cash said all cool and calm high off the weed.

"Oh yeah, hey what's going on?" Pinky asked thinking back on the other night when she met the too ugly ass trick that called himself Cash.

"Shit just chilling. Trying to see what you getting into tonight."

Pinky had heard this line plenty of times before. She knew this nigga was trying to fuck so she played right along now determined to get in Cash pockets.

"I got to go shake my ass at this fuck ass club tonight, rent due and my shoe fetish done set me back like hell," Pinky lied as she bobbed her head to the Young Jeezy blasting from her car speakers.

"Shiiiit…look this the move, come on out to the Super 8 on MLK and I'll take care of your rent," Cash said hoping the thick, fine, white Pinky would agree.

"Man my rent 1500 dollars," Pinky said then paused to see how Cash would reply.

Cash knew she was lying but he was set on getting some of

Pinky tonight.

"No problem I got you. I am in room 241," Cash said nonchantly, as he reached over and grabbed his sack of purp off the hotel room nightstand.

"Ok that'll work—you drinking on something?" Pinky asked, knowing she would have to be drunk and high to fuck ugly ass Cash.

"Nah, pickup a bottle of that Remy. I got some killer purp already," Cash said calmly, but really feeling the effects of the purp.

"Ok, I am on my way," Pinky said exiting the highway and changing directions in route to the liquor store, then off to the hotel for the night.

Cash was laid up in the hotel room waiting for Pinky when his phone rang.

"Yeah," Cash answered not recognizing the number on the caller display.

"What up G, you played the wrong nigga now…"

"Who's this? What the fuck you talking 'bout. This is Turk?"

"Nigga you know…"

"Boy, I told you that was that thang! I know you ready to grab a couple more of that good shit," Cash said with emphasis, so high he missed Turk's threat.

Turk was confused but decided to play along. As Cash talked he got madder by the seconds, he really felt this Atlanta nigga Cash thought he was slow.

"Nigga, how you know? Boy I need two more right now. I know it's late but I got to make this lick. Nigga's hitting me with twenty nine a piece," Turk lied as he held his breath hoping Cash would bite.

"Nigga you fam its all good just come by the Super 8 on MLK, I'm in room 241. I will have you ready," Cash said eagerly not trying to miss no money.

"Aight, I will be out there," Turk replied as he loaded his twelve gauge pistol grip, the one he planned to use to blow Cash head off tonight for almost getting him killed with the fake dope.

"Bet that, I will holla."

"True dat," Turk said, as he pulled his black hoodie from his closet.

Pinky sang Jeezy's *"Thug Motivation"* verse by verse in route to the hotel room. She smiled, thanking God for the trick nigga Cash.

Chapter 60

The next morning Bay Bay's death was the talk of the prison. A lot of his crew had come together to avenge his death but they wasn't for sure who was behind his murder.

Real got ready for war as soon as he raised up out of the bed. He grabbed his tool from the heater where it had been hid every since he left. Putting on his state jacket and skull cap he tucked the shank in his waist and headed downstairs.

"126 bottom to the barbershop," Real gave the old white gay officer that was working the dorm his room number and bunk location so he could sign him out to the barbershop.

"They ain't called barbershop yet," the gay officer said, like an agitated female.

"I need to go get me a haircut for my visit this weekend! They don't never call us!" Real snapped. "Just sign me out to the store," Real said trying to get out of the dorm by any means.

"Haven't called store either," the gay officer said, rolling his eyes.

Just as Real was about to snap the dorm intercom sounded.

"Store call for the east yard! East yard report to the store," the officer in main control screamed over the loud speakers.

"Sign me out, 126 bottom.," Real said as he stepped outside of the dorm door and onto the compound.

Just as Real was making his way down the sidewalk he saw Tino coming out of the hole with about ten other inmates. Glad to see Tino he rushed over and gave him some dap.

"What's up bro! Free at last!" Real said as he helped Tino carry his property to his assigned dorm.

"Not for long these bitch niggas got to pay. As soon as I can grab my piece we going to crank this bitch up I'm going to make sure they put me on the bus. I'm ready to leave this bitch anyway," Tino said with malice as him and Real reached his dorm.

While Real waited in the doorway Tino put his property in his room and made a stop in one of his long time Mexican friend's room. He adjusted the eight inch razor homemade knife that he had under his shirt as he exited back out the room.

"We going to hit the west yard first and holla at my nigga Yaki, he riding with us," Tino said as they walked briskly across the yard.

"Bet," Real said with nothing but killing on his mind.

Real had lost everything that meant something to him. Right now he didn't care if he lived or died, he felt as he had nothing to live for. As him and Tino walked across the yard to their surprise Yaki was coming through the gate with a couple of his goons in tow.

"Bro! Nigga we was just on the way over to holla at you. We 'bout to set this bitch off. Oh, this my nigga Real, the one they pulled that on," Tino said as they pulled over into the corner by the gate.

"What up fam," Yaki said with a heavy southern drawl.

"What up bro," Real replied looking up at the muscle bound giant of a man that had tattoos all over his face.

"Where these bitches lay? It's time to do what it do," Yaki called out alerting the two menacing men that never spoke only followed him.

"The nigga Scram and Third Born is in H-building. OG is in J-building. They the main ones behind this shit! If any one of their banger bitches step up we laying them flat," Tino spat as they started in H-building direction.

"Old man Reddick working the building you know he love them Georgia Bulldogs, Lil Doodie pull him out and keep his busy so we can get by him," Yaki told his lil goon.

As they reached the dorm old man Reddick was standing in the doorway chewing on some tobacco. Lil Doodie pulled up on him and started barking like a dog.

"What about them dogs!" Doodie called out as he got up and close to the officer.

"Yeahhhh doggie! Them dogs did it again! Boy you too young to really know about them dogs," Reddick called out stepping outside the dorm on the sidewalk.

"What! Man I go way back! All the way back to them Hershel Walker days," Doodie said trying to hold the officer's attention.

"You might know a lil something. Did you see them light up Georgia Tech," Reddick asked now fully engulfed in the conversation.

Officer Reddick was so caught up in the football conversation that he didn't notice the four men walk into his dorm. As the men walked across the floor they asked where Scram was but before anyone could answer Tino spotted him sitting upstairs on a trashcan outside his room door listening to his CD player. Scram didn't notice the men until they were running up the steps in his direction.

"Shit!" Scram called out as he snatched off his CD player headphones and tried to run.

Real reached out and grabbed him as he tried to get away. Just as Real was grabbing him Yaki was pulling his ice pick out. Real wrapped his arm around Scrams neck and threw him around like a rag doll. Yaki didn't waste time sticking him in the chest, neck, and face as Real held him wide open for the punishment.

"No..Plea...Ahh!" Scram tried to scream but Real's hold wouldn't permit.

The whole dorm looked on in surprise. Third Born stepped

out of his room to see what all the commotion was about. At first sight Tino wasted no time rushing him. As soon as Third Born saw what was going on, he tried to step back in his room and close the door. It was too late, Tino had caught him before he could get away.

"Smack!" Tino slapped him first just to get his attention.

"Please! I'm sorry," A scared Third Born yelled as he shook uncontrollably.

As he screamed out Tino pulled his knife. Yaki's other goon beat Tino to the punch as he hit Third Born with his homemade tool in the neck and head repeatedly. As soon as Third Born hit the floor Tino kicked and stomped him in the face. He laid there in a puddle of blood shaking as they stepped around him.

Real and Yaki had did the muthafucker to Scram. He had holes in so many places it would take forever to plug him up. Real and Yaki calmly walked back down the stairs as Tino and Yaki's goon followed. Seeing old man Reddick still caught up in the football conversation they eased back out in route to see OG. Lil Doodie cut the conversation off suddenly and followed.

"The bitch Miss Johnson working the dorm I got her," Real said as he pulled up first.

"What up lady I still got that shit got crazy but as soon as I get back situated I'm going to hit you," Real said in a cool tone.

"Yeah ok I heard about what happened," she replied still drunk over the man that stood before her.

"Look we need to holla at my people OG for a second," Real told her not giving her a chance to refuse as they all entered the dorm.

Tino knew exactly where OG room was being that he used to be in this same dorm. As they walked through the dorm they saw a lot of officers running to H building with a medical cart following. Knowing that their time was limited they pounced on OG's room.

OG was laying in the bed half sleep when he door flew open.

Turning over to see who was coming in his room he was hit square in the face by Yaki.

"Ahh! Wha..! Sto..!" He stuttered as Real moved in and snatched him out the bed and slammed him against the locker in the small confined room.

"What's up young blood! Please yall don't hurt me! The Chaplain put the hit out!" OG screamed like a bitch.

All the men in the room looked at each other at the mention of the Chaplain.

"What the fuck you mean the Chaplain?" Real spat as he wedged his forearm in OG's neck.

"Man I swear the chaplain giving a half million for yo life ! He pulled me and…"

That's all Real needed to hear. He knew who was in contact with the Italians. Releasing OG from his forearm grip he stepped back as Tino pulled up on OG with his knife in hand. Real heard the man scream as Tino and Yaki went to work on him with their tools. Real rushed by Miss Johnson who tried to stop him to talk.

"I will get at you tonight," Real lied as he rushed out the dorm in route to the chaplains office.

The whole compound was going crazy. After Yaki, Tino and the goons exited OG's room with blood covered clothes Miss Johnson got on her radio and called a 10/10 knowing what had just happened.

The compound was in an uproar. Lockdown was called as officers from everywhere rushed J building. It wasn't enough medical personnel to handle all the bloodshed. Just as Tino, Yaki and the two goons were headed across the yard the CERT team pounced on them after seeing all the blood on their clothes. They knew then that they had their men.

"Get down now!" They yelled as they rushed them in the middle of the yard.

To their surprise the men didn't get down instead they pulled their weapons and went full blast at the approaching officers.

Chapter 61

" *K*nock! Knock!"

Cash jumped up off the hotel room bed and peeked out of the curtain. He saw it was Pinky all dressed up in pink Baby Phat gear.

"What up sexy," Cash said as he opened the door to let her in.

"Hey," Pinky said as she stepped into the room with a bottle of Remy tucked in her arm. "Damn that sticky all in the air, pass it nigga," Pinky demanded playfully as she sniffed the air.

"I was just about to roll another blunt. Here you take care of that while I fix this Remy up," Cash said passing her the bag of weed and blunts while grabbing the bottle from her.

After thirty minutes of drinking and smoking Cash and Pinky were high as a kite and feeling real good. Cash wasted no time reaching over grabbing on the thick fine Pinky.

"Hold up where the money for my rent?" Pinky slurred as she grabbed Cash hand.

"Damn shawty you tripping on that lil money, I got you," Cash spat, as he resumed his fondling.

"Where the money!" Pinky snapped this time causing Cash to get mad.

Jumping up out of the bed Cash reached under the bed and

grabbed the whole bag of money.

"Bitch I got money! Matter of fact here go a stack extra!" Cash screamed as he threw a wad of money at a now satisfied Pinky.

"Damn nigga quit tripping and come get this pussy!" Pinky screamed calming Cash down watching him slide the money back under the bed.

Cash wasted no time getting him and Pinky naked. Disregarding a rubber he dived into Pinky's dripping wet pussy raw with no regards. Cash pinned her legs back and fucked Pinky like a mad man. He gripped her c-cups tight while he hopped up and down inside the screaming, hurting Pinky. Cash didn't know the meaning of gentle. Pinky screamed to the top of her lungs when Cash thrusted his rock hard dick into her ass unannounced. Cash put his hand over her mouth while he fucked her hard in the ass. Seeing the white girl claw at the bed and screaming turned Cash on. The alcohol and weed had Cash zoned out; so zoned out that he didn't hear Turk at the door.

Turk tried the knob but saw the door was locked. Listening in he heard a female yelling. Then he heard Cash. Turk knocked harder this time getting Cash's attention.

"Hold up!" Cash screamed knowing it was Turk coming for the dope.

Turk didn't respond he just stood at the door patiently waiting. He decided not to enter the room at all because the woman would be a potential witness to what he was about to do to Cash. Turk would wait for Cash to open the door and blow him away with the pistol grip pump. As Cash got out the bed he told Pinky to get the door.

Cash pulled two kilos from the bag of dope he had wedged under the bed. Pinky pulled on his long T-shirt and headed to the door to let the unexpected visitor in. Just as Pinky pulled the door open a loud blast sounded. When Cash looked up he saw half of Pinky's head explode.

"Shit!" Cash yelled as he jumped across the bed and grabbed

his pistol.

Pinky's perfect body crumpled to the floor lifeless with her brains hanging out. Cash came up blasting refusing to be a statistic but Turk was long gone. Turk cursed himself for reacting so quickly, he was sure that Cash would open the door. Turk now had to regroup and lay low until it was time to strike again.

Cash was going crazy. He packed up all the money and dope and ran out the hotel room. He fumbled with his keys as he got in the car. He sped out of the parking lot and into the busy street. As he rode down the main road he tried to figure out Turk's position. After dismissing the thought he put his plan together to kill Turk. Pulling up at the stop light Cash took a deep breath. Just as he was about to pull off his passenger side window shattered. The buck shots from the twelve gauge entered the car striking him all at once. The pain was unbearable. Cash was barely living when he heard another blast. Everything went dark.

Turk had decided to lay on Cash. He knew Cash would come out the hotel sooner than later. Pulling out the parking lot behind him he waited for the perfect time to finish the job. Now that Cash was taken care of he could rest. It was hard for him to sleep knowing the wanna be slick ass Atlanta nigga had got down on him.

Chapter 62

*R*eal reached the chaplains office and walked right in. The chaplain knew what Real was there for as soon as he saw him enter.

"There's no need for violence please let me explain." The chaplain said calmly hoping to keep Real at ease.

"You right but you playing by my rules now. I know you in contact with the people that want me dead. There's only one condition that I don't kill you right here and now. I want you to call the Italians and tell them I'm dead and to deposit the money into this account." Real said as he scribbled his offshore account number down that he kept hidden for emergencies.

"I can't lie to…"

Before he could get his words out Real was on him with the shank pointed at his neck.

"Ok! Ok!" The chaplain said as he picked up the phone.

Two minutes later he was reading off the account number to the Michael. Michael smiled as he hung up the phone with the chaplain and called Angelo.

"Mission complete!" Real is dead and I just texted you the account to deposit the money." Michael said excitedly happy to have carried out the bosses order.

"Good job Michael, now I know my uncle can rest in

peace."Angelo said as he hung up the phone.

Angelo was now satisfied that revenge had been administered. His man Blanco had been paid off for his work on Constance and now he was about to deposit the money for the work on Real. Angelo smiled as he kicked his feet up on the desk and pulled a Cuban cigar from his jacket pocket.

* * * * *

Real waited for the Chaplain to hang up the phone before he finished him off. The chaplain lifeless body was found the next day with a shank hanging out his neck. After the altercation and stand-off, Tino, Yaki, and the goons were transferred to a maximum security lockdown unit . Real slipped through the cracks but was still transferred a week later to a minimum security prison where he plotted his revenge on the Italians and B-low.

A month after arriving at the minimum security prison the counselor called Real into her office and handed him an envelope. Pulling out the letter and reading it made Real smile.

"Congratulations! I don't want to see you back." The counselor told Real as he read his early release papers. Real smiled thinking about the killing that was about to take place in the cities of Atlanta and Miami.

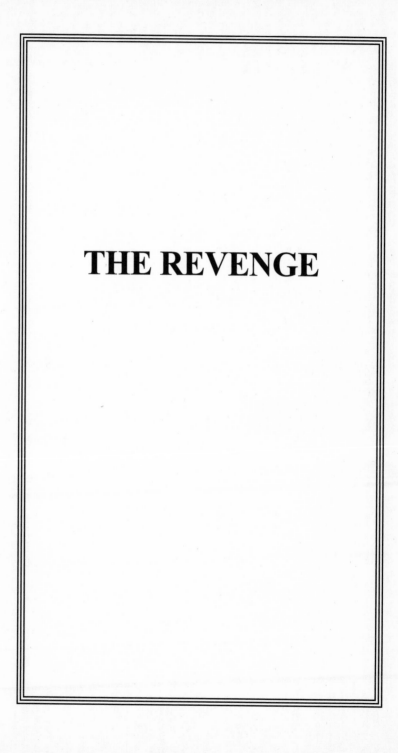

THE REVENGE

Chapter 63

fter getting out of prison Real pulled all the money from his offshore account, moved into a spacious one bedroom loft in downtown Atlanta and bought him a two year old Dodge Charger. He was not concerned with all the luxuries he risked his life for before prison, all he lived for now was revenge.

Pulling up outside his new residence he grabbed the chrome desert eagle that he had recently purchased from one of his old underground connects and tucked it in his waistline. He pulled out his cell phone and made a call as he exited the car, the person on the other line answered in the first ring.

"Hello?"

"You find out where he at?" Real asked the man on the other end of the phone.

"Not yet, but I will be in touch," the man replied and hung up the phone.

Real had been out of prison three weeks now and was tired of waiting on his so called connects to locate the people on his list. He was pretty sure he could track the Italians down with no problem but he would save them for last. Right now, all he wanted was Cash-the snitch and his disloyal lieutenant B-low.

Walking in the house Real went over his plans again; he knew everything had to be done right if he didn't want to return to prison. He pulled out a bag from under the kitchen counter and sat it on the table. The bag contained a black ski mask some black gloves a Kevlar vest and a pair of black army boots, everything he needed to make the people on his list disappear. Real was going to comb the streets of Atlanta every night until they all was located and taken care of then he would end his mission in Miami.

Real often times thought about his baby girl Constance, the only woman he'd ever loved. Constance wasn't like any of the other females he'd met. She was different, and very special. The thing that attracted Real to her was an unseen beauty she possessed inside; a purity he'd longed for, this was his "wifey". Constance gave him hope, she brought out a special side of him—a side of himself he didn't know existed, a side that he only shared with her. The thought of Constance and all his happiness being gone was like his heart had been snatched out of his chest. Knowing the men who'd done this caused Real to feel so enraged; he was a walking time bomb just waiting to explode and cause major damage on any and everybody involved in taking his sweet angel away from him, he didn't care his heart was gone he had no feelings he only wanted revenge and he could taste it. He looked up to the heavens every night and promised her that the person responsible for her death would be found and punished. Real was pretty sure the Italians were responsible, but he knew B-low and Cash were the ones that caused all of his pain. Cash set Real up to go to prison; which took him away from Constance. B-low tried to push up on her causing her to leave the house in the middle of the night while she had killers looking for her. Real held them just as responsible as the man that committed the actual murder. Real pulled a small plastic bag from his pocket and examined the contents. He pulled a knife out of his pocket and stuck it in the bag, when he pulled the knife out of the bag it had a small mountain of the white powder sitting on it. Real leaned over and sniffed the powder off the knife in one long heave. He leaned back in the chair and looked up.

"I'm gonna get them niggas boo, I promise," he whispered as he closed his eyes and meditated.

To be continued...

"Coming Soon"

Lights Out

Other titles from

George Sherman Hudson

Executive Mistress
Drama
Family Ties
Blocked In

"Coming July 2011"
Gangsta Girl Series (ebook)

"Coming 2012"
Drama II
and more...

www.gstreetchronicles.com

G STREET CHRONICLES PRESENTS

A-Town Veteran
Beastmode
Essence of a Bad Girl
Two Face
Dealt the Wrong Hand
Dope, Death & Deception

The Love, Lust & Lies Series
by
Mz. Robinson
Married to His Lies
What We Won't Do for Love

"Coming Fall 2011"
The Lies We Tell for Love
(part 3 of Mz. Robinson's Love, Lust & Lies Series)
Still Deceiving
(part 2 of India's Dope, Death & Deception)

"Coming 2012"
Trap House

**Visit www.gstreetchronicles.com
to view all our titles**

**Join us on Facebook
G Street Chronicles Fan Page**

Name: _____

Address: _____

City/State: _____

Zip: _____

ALL BOOKS ARE $10 EACH

QTY	TITLE	PRICE
	City Lights	
	A-Town Veteran	
	Beastmode	
	Executive Mistress	
	Essence of a Bad Girl	
	Dope, Death and Deception	
	Dealt the Wrong Hand	
	Married to His Lies	
	What We Won't Do for Love	
	Two Face	
	Family Ties	
	Blocked In	
	Drama	
	Shipping & Handling ($4 per book)	

TOTAL $ _____

To order online visit
www.gstreetchronicles.com
Send cashiers check or money order to:
G Street Chronicles
P.O. Box 490082 College Park, GA 30349